My Brother, My Sister, and I

BY YOKO KAWASHIMA WATKINS

SIMON PULSE

First paperback edition April 1996
First Simon Pulse edition November 2002
Copyright © 1994 by Yoko Kawashima Watkins

Simon Pulse
An imprint of Simon & Schuster
Children's Publishing Division
1230 Avenue of the Americas
New York, NY 10020

Also available in a Simon & Schuster Books for Young Readers edition

Designed by Randall Sauchuck
The text of this book was set in Classical Garamond.

Printed and bound in the United States of America
30 29 28 27 26 25 24 23 22

The Library of Congress has cataloged the hardcover edition as follows:

Watkins, Yoko Kawashima.
My brother, my sister, and I / by Yoko Kawashima Watkins.—1st ed.
p. cm.
Sequel to: So far from the bamboo grove.
Summary: Living as refugees in Japan in 1947 while trying to locate their missing father, thirteen-year-old Yoko and her older brother and sister must endure a bad fire, injury, and false charges of arson, theft, and murder.
ISBN 0-02-792526-9
1. World War, 1939–1945—Refugees—Juvenile fiction. [1. World War, 1939–1945—Refugees—Fiction. 2. Japan—Fiction. 3. Refugees—Fiction.] I. Title.

ISBN-13: 978-0-689-80656-8 (Simon Pulse pbk.)
  ISBN-10: 0-689-80656-6 (Simon Pulse pbk.)

IN LOVING MEMORY OF
MY HONORABLE BROTHER HIDEYO

To those I have met through
So Far from the Bamboo Grove,
whose curiosity gave me courage
to go further with my life's story,
my gratitude

With special thanks to Carol B. Chittenden

CONTENTS

PART ONE

Togetherness	2
Fire	19
Moving	33
In the Hospital	43
Morning	53
Blamed	64
At School	75
Loose Morals?	89
At the Police Laboratory	102
Watch Missing	109
Solved	121

PART TWO

Was Father Killed?	135
Silkworms	150
New Year's Eve	158
Silk Thread	170
Shack under the Bridge	184
With the Minatos	201

PART THREE

Twenty Months and One Autumn Day	215
Afterword	227

PART ONE

TOGETHERNESS

Though it was Sunday, I was alone. My brother, Hideyo, had left very early in the morning for the Kyoto city hall, where he stood in line each day trying to get a laborer's job. My sister, Ko, a Seian University student, had gone to work in a department store, sewing kimonos. Before she left, Ko told me to do the cleaning and finish the laundry. "These chores should take Little One all day," she said. I was already thirteen and a half, but Hideyo and Ko still called me by my pet name, Little One.

We only had hot water for supper the night before, so the load of laundry I carried to the stream beyond the clog-factory warehouse where we lived seemed extra heavy. The late-September morning sun was warm on my back, but the stream water was cold. I waded in shin-deep, put our well-worn underwear on a large, flat rock, rubbed it with thin soap, and then beat it clean with a bamboo stick.

While beating, I wondered how I could surprise Hideyo. He was twenty-one years old that day. Though Japanese celebrate their birthdays at the end of the year, how good it would be to surprise him with something nice to eat! But how? For the past few days we had hardly had any food to put in our stomachs. I dipped the underwear into the water to rinse. As I wrung it out, an idea popped into my head. I could go out and sell Ko's wares. Ko sewed kimonos, aprons, and beanbags in her spare time, and she sold these articles to make money for food.

Wildflowers grew on the pebbly bank where I spread the clothes to dry. After weighting them down with heavy rocks, I ran back to the warehouse. Cleaning was easy. Only a four-tatami-mat room,* eleven stairway steps, and a small, dark entrance hall. The noon streetcar passed and shook the entire warehouse as I was finishing the cleaning. Because we owned no clock, we depended on the streetcar to tell time.

We used an apple box in the far-right corner of the room as an altar for the mess-kit urn that held Mother's ashes. Before I left, I bowed and asked Mother to protect our family treasure, the ancestors' sword that we had placed next to the urn. I also asked Mother to wish me luck with my sales. Mother had been dead for almost two years now.

I locked both doors of the warehouse, front and back, and headed toward the main street of town along the streetcar track. Carrying Ko's handicrafts in a small wrapping cloth, I went door-to-door. My stomach kept growling with hunger. Then, too, walking in my faded, flapping red leather shoes was a labor. For each step I

---

*Each tatami mat is three by six feet, two inches thick, made of sweet-smelling straw.

took, I had to lift my left foot higher than my right. But these were the only shoes I owned.

At the town's barbershop, I ducked to see the clock through the glass window. It was almost three o'clock. So far I had only sold six beanbag toys. In my wrapping cloth there were still two baby kimonos, three bibs, and a housewife's apron. I wanted to sell everything.

As I went along, I could not help but think back on the happy days with Father and Mother in Nanam, Korea. We lived in a beautiful big house with many different-sized tatami-mat rooms. Our home was surrounded by a graceful bamboo grove. My stomach was always filled with good food. I had plenty of clothes to wear and several pairs of fine shoes.

However, just before midnight on July 29, 1945, Mother, Ko, and I had to flee. We had learned from a friend in the Japanese army, Corporal Matsumura, that the Communists were about to attack our town. Father was away in Manchuria, and Hideyo was working in an ammunition factory twenty miles from home. We left Father and Hideyo a note asking them to meet us at the train station in Seoul. While we were fleeing to safety in the south, an airplane dropped a bomb and I was thrown into the air. This incident left me deaf in my right ear, and also with constant back pain. Until we reached Seoul, we lived on leaves from bushes and what Ko found on Korean farmland. When we arrived in Seoul, we learned that atom bombs had been dropped on Nagasaki and Hiroshima, and that Japan had lost World War II. The Korean peninsula was divided in half and the Communists had taken over the north. We could never go back to our home in the bamboo grove. We had become refugees.

All around us, people were suffering from wounds, hunger, and homelessness. It was normal to see people sleeping under bridges or anywhere they found space. We always had to guard what little we had from thieves and bums. Once, at a train station in Korea, a man ordered us to make room for him to sleep. He was about to attack Mother. Then Ko pulled out her peeling knife and almost plunged it into his throat. He left us alone.

When we reached Japan, I found the homeland I'd dreamed of shattered by war. We made our way to Kyoto, which had not been bombed. Here, greatly weakened by our struggle, Mother died suddenly at the train station. It was a terrible blow, but Ko did not allow me to become a crybaby. She pushed me to live. We made our home over the clog-factory warehouse in a town outside of the city. On weekends, we searched for Father and Brother by posting their names on the refugee-center walls in Maizuru, where cargo boats brought back refugees from Korea and Manchuria. We often gathered food from garbage bins in the alleys, behind the inns. Ko polished shoes and sold her handicrafts on the street to earn our daily rice.

Here in the Kyoto area, the inhabitants had never experienced the horror of war, and most of them treated us as outsiders. I hated going to Sagano Girls' School because everybody picked on me. They called me Rag Doll or Trash Picker. Because I had no notebooks, I collected crumpled papers from the classroom wastepaper basket and smoothed out the wrinkles. Many of the papers had little writing and all were blank on one side. Once, one of the girls made an airplane with a piece of notebook paper and aimed it at me. "You want more paper?" she yelled. The other girls laughed. Another girl made a huge drawing of me with my rucksack picking up trash in the furnace room of the school. Under the drawing was written: DEMOCRATIC SYSTEM! PRESTIGIOUS SAGANO ACCEPTS TRASH PICKER AS STUDENT.

To live for today and tomorrow was hard enough, but the intimidation at school made my life so miserable that there were times I wished I were dead! But miracles happen. Our brother, Hideyo, finally joined Ko and me in the spring of 1946.

I was extremely happy to have Hideyo home; but my heart was still empty, my chest tightened, and I swallowed big lumps whenever I thought of Father. He was an Oxford graduate, tall and broad-shouldered, with thick black hair, and his posture was always straight and most distinguished-looking. When I was a child, he was always ready to help me. He told us stories at suppertime with delightful gestures. He never failed to tell Mother how good the evening meal was, gently patting her shoulder. Whenever I pleased him, he stroked my back and said merrily, "You have done well!" Even when I did not do well, he still patted my back. Smiling, he'd say, "Go at your own pace. You will achieve eventually. Do not worry." Now we did not know whether Father was dead or alive.

The sun was tilting slowly as I tried a few more houses, earnestly wishing that there would be babies or that the lady of the house would need an apron. No luck.

An old man in dirty work clothes was sitting on the ground near the roadside, cutting the green tops off a mountain of large, white, carrot-shaped radishes called daikons. Seeing fresh, juicy daikons made my mouth water. I wondered if he would sell me a few of the greens. If I had enough money from selling Ko's beanbags, I could make a salad for Hideyo's birthday, and we would be able to go to bed with some food in our stomachs.

I stood there for a while, not knowing what to say. The old man's hands were shaking. He only had two fingers, thumb and index, on his left hand. Every time he slashed greens, his hands shook so badly that I feared he might slash his wrist. He tossed the greens to his left and threw

7

the daikons into one of the large baskets in front of him.

"Good afternoon, sir," I called. The old man paid no attention, but the thought of making Brother a salad for his birthday gave me courage. I went much closer to him. "Good afternoon, sir," I called again. His head was shaking just as badly as his hands.

"Are you working hard, sir?" I asked. He put his shaky left hand to his ear, trying to hear me. I repeated my question loudly and smiled.

"What do you think I am doing?" he said. "Playing? Don't bother me. I am busy. Can't you see?"

The mean old man! My compassion for him faded, but I could see Hideyo clearly in my mind's eye, sitting in front of our apple-box table, devouring fresh daikon-green salad, enjoying his special day.

"Why don't you get some help?" I asked.

"No young people want to help!" He kept on slashing greens.

"Did you ask?"

"Nope! They do not work unless they are paid plenty."

"Can I help?" I asked.

"I cannot pay," he said, still working. I told him I did not wish to be paid, but if he would sell me some greens cheap, I would be glad. The old man looked bewildered.

He told me to sort the daikons. Some were

good and straight, others twisted and oddly shaped. I arranged them neatly in the empty crates by the road and then helped him finish slashing the greens. When the work was done, he said I could take as many of the daikon greens as I wanted, then dump the rest in the compost pit at the end of the vegetable patch.

"Compost pit!" I yelled. Why, this many greens would keep us alive for weeks! "May I keep all the greens?" I asked.

This time the old man shouted at me. "What are you going to do with them? Beggars would not even eat those!" I told him I wanted to dry them for our meals. "How are you going to carry them back home?" he asked.

"Right now, I only want to have enough for tonight's supper, but I will come back with my brother to get the rest tomorrow," I answered happily.

After I loaded the daikon boxes onto his cart for him, the old man said he would get home earlier because of my unexpected help. When he stood up, he stretched his back and rubbed his hips with both hands.

"Does your back hurt?" I asked. There was throbbing pain in my back from sitting on the damp ground while slashing the greens.

He said, "Young as you are, you have no idea of an aching back."

I almost shouted, "I *do*," but the joy of getting the daikon greens kept me quiet.

Then the old man reached into the cart and handed me six twisted daikons. "Customers will never buy these," he said. "For you, young maiden!" I bowed deeply, thanking him for the unexpected kindness. "You earned them," he said bluntly. His toothless smile told me that he was not the mean old man I'd imagined. I told him, "No matter how late, I will return tomorrow to get the greens, so do not dump them in the compost pit!" The old man nodded his shaky head. I already saw myself fixing salad for my family as I flew home.

We owned no large pot, so I used a water bucket to cook the daikon greens. While waiting for the water to boil on the campfire stove Ko had made outside the warehouse, I ran to the stream bank and gathered all of our laundry.

Daylight was fading now, and I had to move fast. I rushed back to the warehouse and folded the laundry quickly. I took the greens and one fat daikon to rinse in the stream water. While rinsing I ate a couple of pieces of the hairy greens raw, for I was starving.

As I was returning to the warehouse, I glimpsed a short, stout man walking on the narrow path between the factory and the warehouse. I could not see him clearly. "Honorable Brother?" I called. There was no answer. When the man slipped away to the other side of the factory, I became frightened. Ever since we had become refugees, I had had a fear of strange men.

We had stayed in places where young girls were raped and often killed in the dark. I had seen brutality many times. With trembling legs I rushed back to where the water was boiling. My mouth was getting dry and my heart was pounding.

Mr. and Mrs. Masuda, the factory owners, lived in a house across the streetcar tracks. Mrs. Masuda had been at the Kyoto station searching for her niece, Junko, when Mother died. She had offered us a place to stay, and in exchange for our room we watched the warehouse for robbers. I stretched my neck to see if there was a light on, but the house was dark. The Masudas weren't due to return from Tokyo until sometime that evening.

Wishing Hideyo or Ko would come, I put a long stick in the fire to burn the tip. If the man came around to attack me, I thought I would hit him with the burning stick or throw boiling water at him. While cooking the greens, I kept looking to see if the man was there. When the wind flipped and flapped small bits of sticks or scrap materials around the factory, I thought I heard his footsteps.

My hands were shaking as I scooped up the greens with chopsticks. I laid them on the strainer Hideyo had made from narrow bamboo strips. When they were cool, I tried to lay them straight on a wooden board to chop, but I could not do it with my trembling hands. I could barely arrange the greens on a large oblong, wood scrap. We had no money to buy ceramic platters or rice bowls, so we used discarded wood scraps from the factory as plates.

I saved the greenish water to drink as soup. I could not slice the daikon as thin as I wanted because my hands would not behave. But I piled the crunchy daikon around the greens and covered the wooden platter with large bamboo leaves. After hiding it with the rest of the daikons behind the stairway, I quickly went upstairs where I felt safer. Then after respectfully removing Mother's ashes and the sword from the apple box, I made a table and arranged our chopsticks for our meal.

When I heard Ko yell "I am home," I rushed down and told her that an unfamiliar man was around the factory building. "Maybe it was Mr. Masuda," Ko said, hanging her rucksack on a nail. She looked tired.

"No! Mr. Masuda is handicapped. He cannot walk unless he has crutches," I exclaimed. "Besides, they are not home yet. Whoever it was, he did not have crutches, and when I called, 'Honorable Brother?' he did not answer me."

"You say you cannot see the blackboard in school. How can you see a man walking around the factory?"

"I saw him! I saw someone walking! I did not see his face. He was short and stout. That's why I thought he was Brother!" I was disgusted with Ko for doubting me. "Besides," I said, talking back to her, "I did not say I cannot see the *blackboard*; I only said, I have a hard time seeing the teacher's writing on the blackboard!"

"Don't talk back at me. Where is your respect for your elders?" Ko gave me a nasty look.

I almost snapped, "You are only five years older than me. You are not my mother," but I bit my tongue.

"Let me go take a look," grumbled Ko. I told her to take the burning stick from the fire, in case he was still there. "What you saw was probably a shadow of the maple tree by the building," Ko insisted. But she took the stick.

The greenish, watery soup in the bucket was hot. I took hold of the bucket handle and stood there, prepared. If the worst came, I was going to run and throw hot soup at the man.

Ko screamed! Almost at the same time a man's voice came from the outhouse. I ran with the bucket. Ko was dashing toward the warehouse. As the hot soup splashed on my legs, the edge of my flapping shoe got caught on a rock and I almost fell flat. Ko shoved me into the warehouse. Breathless, she checked the front and back doors. In the twilight her face was pale.

Ko took a big breath. She said she had gone around the factory and seen no one. Since she had gone that far, she decided to use the toilet. (Japanese toilets were like American outhouses.) As she was about to open the door, a man leaped out. Screaming, Ko hit out at the man with the burning stick, and he yelled. She feared he would chase her.

When Ko's hard breathing calmed, she asked me why I was holding the hot-water bucket. "To protect you," I said. "It's our soup." Still troubled, Ko did not see it was green.

"Soup? I did not come home with miso or soy sauce. I cannot make you soup tonight," said Ko. She'd worked all day to finish a garment, but she would not be paid until after it had been delivered to the customer.

"Today is our brother's birthday," Ko said in a sad tone. She brought a handful of apple and tangerine peelings from her bag. They were wrapped in newspapers. She said she had picked them out of a wastepaper basket before leaving the department store.

Ko wanted to wash the fruit peelings at the stream, but she did not dare go outside. She scooped some greenish hot water from the bucket to wash the peelings in an old cooking pot that Mrs. Masuda had loaned us. "What is this?" she said when she noticed the color of the water.

I told her I had cooked some vegetable greens and saved the water for soup. She asked where I'd gotten vegetable greens. I said, "A good thing happened at the roadside today," and I tried to smile, but I could hear my own frightened heartbeats.

"Didn't I tell you to stay at home and finish the laundry? You are not obedient!" Ko was angry.

"I obeyed!" I yelled. She thought I was still a tiny child! Sometimes Ko got on my nerves. "I finished the cleaning and did our laundry."

Hideyo was pounding at the back door to be let in. "Why are you standing here in the dark, looking like ghosts?" he asked. "Why don't you turn on the light?"

Ko waved her arm in the air to reach the string to pull on the light. A twenty-five–watt bulb lit the entrance.

Hideyo looked exhausted. I told him about the strange man I had seen and Ko told him about the man she'd hit with the fire stick. Hideyo said he would investigate before he washed himself in the stream. He said the lights were on at the Masudas' house, and that Ko should go and tell them about the stranger. He asked me to bring him a blanket to wrap up in after his cold bath. There was no soap. I had used it all doing the laundry.

While Ko went to the Masudas' house, I put the bucket back on the fire to reheat the soup. I took the large wooden platter full of sliced daikons and cooked greens upstairs, wishing we had brighter light. I'd grumbled once that the Masudas should give us a sixty-watt bulb for the upstairs, instead of forty, so that I could study better. But Ko sternly said, "Never complain!"

On the apple-box table I arranged the platter of daikons and our tired-looking wooden soup bowls. The bowls and the sword had journeyed with us all the way from our home in the bamboo grove.

I went down to the fire. The greenish water was boiling and so I brought the bucket upstairs. Using my own wooden soup bowl as a ladle, I poured the green daikon water into Hideyo's and Ko's bowls. Ko returned, slamming the warehouse's front door to close it tightly. Hideyo came upstairs wrapped in a blanket. Ko followed, saying she had put the teapot on the fire for apple-tangerine tea. When they saw the spread on the apple-box table, their mouths hung open for a few seconds.

"Happy Birthday, Honorable Brother!" I smiled. Ko also greeted him.

Hideyo grinned. He said he had been digging the ground with a pick all day and his head felt like a puffy fish. The sounds of the picks still rang in his ears and he was so tired that he hadn't realized it was his birthday. He slowly drank the steamy green soup, which he pronounced, "Deeeeelightful!" He slowly ate the soft greens. The aroma of apple-tangerine tea came from outside, making our humble dining cheerful, but I was scared that someone might be peeking into the warehouse.

"Did you see anyone while you were bathing?" I asked.

"No one," said Hideyo, biting a crunchy daikon. "Did you tell the Masudas about the suspicious man, Ko?" asked Hideyo.

"Mrs. Masuda took off for the police station right away," said Ko as she swallowed the soup. When I heard her say *police,* I relaxed.

"Now, Little One," Ko began eagerly, "I want to know what happened at the roadside."

I told them about my meeting with the old man. After ending my story, I asked Hideyo and Ko to go with me to get the daikon greens before the next day's supper. "I will tie the greens together and dry them over bamboo sticks for winter."

"You are amazing, Little One," Hideyo said. He patted my back as Father used to do when I pleased him. "I never expected a fine birthday treat! Thanks!"

I told Hideyo I had wanted to buy some rice and miso to make him a good supper. "If there was no war, we would not have to suffer like this. Everything would be heavenly. Father and Mother would be . . ." My voice trembled and I could not finish. I wanted to say that Father and Mother would be very happy to see their son become twenty-one.

Hideyo looked at me seriously. "The word *if* is hindsight. Hindsight is stupid. If we knew the outcome of things to come, we probably would not do them, or, we would do them differently." He said, "Accept what has happened. We must move forward with Kawashima spirit, until Father returns. You hear?"

I nodded, but I was already sniffling, missing Mother and Father. At the same time, I looked at Hideyo in surprise. I remembered he had been a very mischievous boy. He gave Mother many headaches in Nanam. Now he was talking like Father.

While Hideyo went to check around the warehouse and the factory once more, Ko and I went to the stream to wash our eating utensils. She dumped some water over the cooking fire. Smoke from the ashes rose and made me cough, so I ran upstairs with the bowls still wet.

I put the apple-box table back in the far-right corner. Using both hands, I carefully picked up the urn from the floor. Though it was wrapped in Mother's bath towel, the mess kit we used as an urn had been badly banged during our long, frightening journey, and the lid would not fit. I moved slowly because I did not want to spill Mother's ashes. With deep respect, I placed the urn and the sword on the apple-box altar. I stored the eating utensils in the side opening of the box, then spread our futons.* Usually I slept at the far end near the altar, but not tonight. I put my futon between Ko and Hideyo to feel safer.

Hideyo crawled into his and stretched. "Ah! It was a good day. I worked. It was a super day to go to bed with food in my tummy!" He yawned.

I lay flat on my stomach in my futon, trying to memorize spelling for English class.

Nights were cold in the warehouse, so I did

---

*Three-inch-thick foldable cotton-filled mattresses

not bother to take off my blouse and wartime trousers. We had no pajamas. Ko sat on her futon bed and began sewing a baby kimono to sell. Hideyo's snores soon told us he was asleep.

The last streetcar of the day passed, shaking the entire warehouse. It was half past twelve. Knowing a streetcar would wake us up at half past five in the morning, I lay down. I folded my hands on my chest and prayed, "Father, please stay alive and come home." Ko put her sewing things away. As soon as she crawled into her futon and covered us with blankets and futon comforters, I pasted myself to her to get warm and wished I could meet Father, at least in my dreams.

FIRE

I woke up suddenly, feeling terribly thirsty. I had never felt such heat before in the warehouse. I could not breathe. The room was wrapped in smoke. I sat up on the futon, with my eyes burning. Flames were blazing outside the little window.

"Fire! Fire!" I screamed. Both Hideyo and Ko jumped up. The clog factory was on fire and the blaze was touching the warehouse! Hideyo waved his hand in the air to find the string to pull the light switch. The light did not go on.

"I'll drop everything down the stairs!" Hideyo yelled. "Ko and Little One, go down! Quickly, quickly! Drag our belongings to the front street!"

I ran down the stairs. The fire had already spread to the back entrance of the warehouse. I opened the front door and began to throw our possessions onto the street. Ko rushed down to help me. Hideyo kept on dropping things down the staircase: futons, blankets, Ko's sewing box, and our school things. The cool air fed the flame and it rose upstairs. I heard Hideyo coughing badly. The blaze spread toward the stairs. I remembered my five daikons and I ran to get them.

"Honorable Brother! Come down! Fast!" screamed Ko. The town firemen arrived with their hand water-pump carts. The firemen and town volunteers worked quickly, trying to extinguish the fire in the warehouse. In the light of the blaze many people stood, watching.

Suddenly Ko shouted. "Mother's ashes, sword, wrapping-cloth bundle!" Just as Hideyo ran out, Ko vanished inside. She was so fast, Hideyo could not stop her. "Don't go up!" I screamed at the top of my voice. Hideyo ran to catch Ko, but he was stopped by the policemen. I chased after Ko, too, but I was held tightly by a volunteer fireman. My stomach churned to think of my sister burning to death in the blaze. I kept screaming Ko's name.

Ko had gone up for the ashes, the sword, and the wrapping-cloth bundle containing Mother's and our summer clothes, sweaters, overcoats, socks, and few pieces of underwear. In the bundle's secret pocket was Father's name seal, Nanam school documents, our family's important papers, and some cash Mother had saved. Ko had carried it on her back in the Korean war zone. She had carried it in wind, rain, and heat. She had carried it everywhere until we had settled here.

Hideyo, still held by policemen, was trying hard to get away from them. He kept on screaming at Ko to come down. Two firemen wearing helmets strained to pump the water faster. The other two aimed the fire hose upstairs where Ko had gone. Ko dropped the wrapping-cloth bundle down the stairs. Hideyo pulled away from the policemen and rushed to drag it out onto the street. The spray from the hose drenched me. A fireman ordered me to go to a safer place. I fought with him. "Sister Ko!" I screamed, looking up the stairs.

The blaze had reached our room. I was crying aloud for Ko. Hideyo was screaming for our sister and struggling to go upstairs, but he was held back. In the flames I saw Ko at the top of the stairs, holding something to her chest, wanting to come down but trying to avoid the fire.

Then she fell, face down, from the top of the stairs onto the concrete floor below. Her blouse was burning. I tore away from the volunteer fireman and threw myself over her. Hideyo jumped and covered both of us. The firemen streamed water on us to put out our burning clothes.

"Honorable Sister!" I cried. She did not move. I shook her shoulders and Ko let out an agonizing moan. In her arms were Mother's ashes in the mess kit and our precious family treasure, the sword. Hideyo pulled me up away from Ko and two volunteers carefully put her on a stretcher.

Ko was unconscious, but occasionally she moaned in pain as Hideyo slowly took the sword and the urn from her arms. He and some volunteers were going to carry Ko to Dr. Yamada, two miles away.

Before Hideyo left, he handed me the sword and said that if someone tried to bother me I should chase him away. Brother grinned, "You are a maiden samurai." He untied the wrapping-cloth bundle and gently put the urn between Mother's clothes. Tying up the bundle he said, "The policemen will be on guard, but until I return, stay where you are!"

"Is Honorable Sister going to die?" I asked. I could not stop the tears.

"No! No, Little One! Sister is too tough to die!"

"Let's go!" a volunteer commanded. Hideyo and three other men got hold of the wooden stretcher handles and lifted Ko. They quickly walked off.

"You cannot die, Honorable Sister! You just cannot!" I screamed. I threw myself onto the wrapping-cloth bundle and begged Mother to protect her dutiful daughter, my only sister in this whole wide world.

I was so worried about Ko that I did not realize how soaking wet I was. I was barefoot and shivering. I tried to untie the wrapping-cloth bundle to get a sweater and a pair of socks, but Hideyo had tied it very tightly, and the knot would not loosen. I covered myself in a dampened blanket. Fleecy and white when we escaped from the bamboo grove, now it had turned completely gray, with dark bloodstains. I sat still and leaned on the bundle, holding the sword against my chest. My legs were burning and I remembered the hot soup splashing when I had run to Ko with the bucket early that evening.

Once the fire was out, the spectators went away. There were no stars in the sky. The Masudas' house was dark. Strange, I thought. Why haven't they come to check on their warehouse and see how we are?

"How are you doing?" a man's voice asked. I could not see the man, but only his flashlight, coming near me.

"I am doing well, sir. Thank you," I replied loudly. I was already shivering with cold, but now my whole body trembled in fright. I rewrapped the blanket over my head so that only my face showed, hoping to hide my fear.

When I saw that he was a policeman, I was relieved. But suddenly I remembered the mean army policemen who burst into our house in

Nanam. They robbed us and yanked Mother's gold-framed glasses from her face. Maybe this policeman would try to take our things away too. Beneath the blanket, I put my right hand over the sword. The truth is, I had never pulled the blade from the sheath, and I was not sure how I would manage.

The policeman said, "You are almost on the streetcar tracks. I will help you move your things to the stream bank where it is safe. Soon the first streetcar will pass. It's almost five."

I secured the sword on my trouser belt and started to move things, but my knees were weak and I staggered. The policeman said he would carry the wrapping-cloth bundle for me. But I was cautious. I told him that if he would lift it up and put it on my back, I would be very happy. Ko always carried the bundle because it was heavy. Wet, it was heavier. The tip of the sword's sheath kept hitting my abdomen, making it hard for me to walk, but I reeled along. The policeman walked ahead of me with our futons, shining his flashlight on the rough, pebbly ground so that we could see where we were going.

When he found a good spot, he put the futons down. I bent my knees forward so that I could carefully drop the bundle over the bedding. Instead I fell right onto the ground.

"I offered to bring it," said the policeman, taking the bundle off my back.

"I wanted to carry it. Mother's ashes are in

there," I said, thanking him. He said he would bring the rest of the things for me. I accepted his offer because I was exhausted. But I told him my feet were freezing and I wanted to go back to the warehouse to look for my shoes.

"I will bring them," he said. "There is no need for you to go back to the street."

"They were at the bottom of the steps, where we always took off our shoes."

The policeman returned with the rest of our things wrapped in two blankets, but he did not bring my shoes. "It is wet, dark, and dangerous in there," he said. "When daylight comes I will find them."

The eastern sky began to glow. I could now see the completely burned-out factory and the partly burned warehouse. Only the outhouse was untouched. Mr. and Mrs. Masuda had not come yet.

Two men in white hospital-like gowns were bent low examining something on the burned factory floor, taking notes. One of them occasionally took pictures. Several policemen pounded stakes around the burned buildings and they stretched ropes to keep people from going near.

The first streetcar had passed a long time ago. Now even the third and fourth streetcars had passed by. Still, Hideyo did not come back. What is taking him so long? I wondered. At a slow pace the doctor's office was about thirty minutes from the warehouse. Had Hideyo fainted on the street from exhaustion?

What was happening to Ko? I could not erase from my mind the scene of Ko falling. I could still hear the ominous crack of her bones as she hit the concrete floor. Was she dead? She bossed me around, but now I felt badly for having sassed her before supper. What would I do if both of them never came back? My thoughts raced to Father. Was he still alive? Was I going to be an orphan? Suddenly I felt utterly alone in this huge world, and scared.

If I could talk to Mr. or Mrs. Masuda, I would feel so much better. I was tempted many times to run to their house, but I had to guard what little we possessed. They had to be home; Ko had spoken to them just before supper.

I was hungry, and remembered the five daikons I'd hidden behind the stairway before the fire broke out. The policeman had probably wrapped them in one of the blankets. But there were no daikons in either blanket. He . . . stole . . . my daikons! I was mad! He'd acted kind and helpful, yet had taken food away from me! I walked the few feet to the stream, made a cup with my hands, and drank water. The north wind was strong, but there was faint sunshine among the clouds.

Many people, including housewives with little children and babies on their backs, came and strolled around by the rope. Often they stretched over the rope to see the burned-out factory. The winds carried their voices, but I could not hear what they were saying. The loneliness was terrible.

A boy about five, neatly clothed, ran toward me. Just as I was going to greet him, he grabbed a handful of pebbles and threw them at me. "Beggar! Go away!" he said. I was dumbfounded. At the same time, I was terribly hurt. I had been humiliated by schoolgirls ever since I enrolled at Sagano. Now I must take this insult from a little boy!

I glared fiercely. I wanted to beat him to pieces on the laundry rock with my bamboo stick! Then his mother called in a high-pitched voice, "Son! Don't go near that bum!" Her voice echoed in the open field.

"Go away!" the boy jeered, kicking pebbles at me. I could not take it anymore. I stood up, ready to chase the boy all the way back to his mother. I wanted to tell her to teach her son some manners, but I changed my mind. I remembered what Father said once—"Parents are mirrors of their children"—and I thought, What good would it do? The boy has no model of conduct at home.

Around noon I smelled roasting rice balls. How long had it been since I had eaten rice? My stomach growled and my mouth watered. Maybe I should go to sleep; then I would not be disturbed by the delicious aroma. But I was afraid someone might steal our things if I slept soundly. To keep awake, I went to the stream and washed my face. I looked for a comb in Ko's bag. My heart was filled with pain to think of her and I combed my short hair with deep sighs. Again and again came fresh tears that I could not stop.

To stay awake I spread the dampened blankets and futons out neatly. I even straightened our damp books and papers. Two of our blank post-cards were very wet, and I put them in the sun. I checked what had been rescued from the fire. Besides the wrapping-cloth bundle, we had five canteens. Mother, Ko, and I had each carried two canteens filled with water when we fled home, but I gave one of mine to a woman who was giving birth to a baby on the hospital train. Three mess kits. One was now filled with Mother's ashes. I wished I could untie the bundle's knot and spread the dampened clothes on the ground to dry.

The policeman who had helped the night before came over with a fire inspector, the police chief, a newspaper reporter, and two town offi-cials. The policeman introduced me to them. I was cool, thinking the policeman and his family had eaten my daikons. The police chief asked me questions. How did I discover the fire? Did I see anyone who looked suspicious when the blaze came to the warehouse? Or before? "No," I said, "but I saw a short, stout man wandering around the factory at dusk." Could I identify him?

"No. I am nearsighted, and I only saw his back." I also told them about the man in the outhouse.

"I heard his painful scream," I said to the police chief. "He must have gotten hurt somewhere."

The police chief kept on asking questions. Where did we cook our meals? Had we put out our cooking fire completely? I had not slept all night and I was irritated by his questions. "If we were careless with the cooking fire, the warehouse could burn down," I said. "I saw my sister pouring water on the fire! Do not blame it on us!"

"Where is your sister?" asked the reporter. I wanted to answer him, but all I could do was try not to cry. I bit my lips and stared at him, swallowing the lumps.

"She was injured. Their brother took her to the doctor," said the policeman.

The police chief looked me over from top to bottom. "Where are your parents?" he asked.

"I do not know where my father is, but Mother is in the wrapping cloth. I cannot untie it," I said.

"What?" he shouted. His shout was so loud I jumped. "What do you mean, your mother is in the wrapping cloth? Did you cut her to pieces?"

Everyone roared with laughter. I then realized what I said. I chuckled, but I was terribly embarrassed.

The police chief said it was dangerous for me to stay at the stream bank alone.

"As soon as Brother comes back, we will go," I said. Maybe Mr. and Mrs. Masuda will let us stay in their shed for a while, I thought.

I was uneasy asking, but I could not hold

myself any longer. I asked them to keep their eyes on our things while I went to the outhouse. The inspector said he would first check the toilet. He signaled all clear. Barefoot, I walked lamely on the rough, pebbly ground.

As soon as I returned, the police chief gave me his name card. "Call me, or contact the town police if you see someone suspicious," he said. Then they left me.

I thought I might get some warmth by making a cushion of Ko's blanket to sit on. But the ground was drier than the blanket. I became drowsy. But I must not fall asleep! I must move around. I gathered some wooden scraps. I also gathered large rocks and made a circle. I wanted to build a campfire to heat water-filled canteens. I wanted to drink hot water to warm myself, but I had no paper to build even a small fire.

Suddenly I remembered an old magazine we used in the outhouse. I ran, though I could not run fast on the pebbly bank. I grabbed the magazine and ran back to my spot. I tore several pages and crumpled them to start a fire. No matches! Frustrated, I stabbed at the crumpled paper with a stick. How long must I stay here alone? I wondered.

How was Ko? Not knowing her condition or where Hideyo was drove me wild. Why hasn't Brother come back? I wanted to scream at the top of my lungs to let out the madness inside of me.

A magnifying lens! I remembered. Mr. Naido,

the trash collector at my school, the only friend I had, always saved discarded papers, pencil stubs, rulers, tiny erasers, and whatever else he thought I could use for my learning. I turned my beat-up rucksack inside out and dumped everything onto the blanket. Among all the school items, the magnifying lens fell out. Ah! It was broken to bits. Still, I picked out the biggest pieces. But the afternoon sun was too weak to give out rays strong enough to light a fire.

I thought I could stay awake as long as I kept my mind occupied. So I read my English reader. The more I tried to read, the sleepier I became. I put the book back into the rucksack, and I took out ten sheets of used notebook paper. They were from the classroom wastepaper basket, but the backs were still good. I folded each one of them in half, showing the clean side on top. Using a big-eyed needle I pushed red, white, and black thread through at once and bound the loose ends to make a small tablet. On the front with crayon pieces I drew the Kawashima family crest, a plum blossom of three petals within two circles, and wrote in capital letters, SPELLING.

"Little One!" Hideyo yelled from far away. He was coming from the narrow path between the burned-out factory and warehouse.

I ran to him. "How is Sister? Where is she? Where were you all this time? What took you so long?" I splashed him with questions. How glad I was to see him!

Hideyo said Dr. Yamada had examined Ko and immediately telephoned Kyoto University Hospital in the city. The small town outside of the city limits where we lived did not have an ambulance, so the doctor called a taxi, and Ko was rushed to the hospital. The X ray showed that Ko's right knee was shattered, her left leg was broken in three places, and her right wrist and three ribs were broken. They operated on her without delay.

"Will she be able to walk?" I asked, worrying.

Hideyo swallowed some lumps. His voice quivered. "I certainly hope so. I cannot stand to see her become a cripple." He continued, "Ko must stay in the hospital for a long time." Hideyo was looking off into space, as if remembering the fire scene. "The room was smoky, and I could not see the bundle or the urn and the sword on the apple box. It was my fault," he murmured, trying hard not to cry.

"No! It was not your fault," I said. "She should not have gone up!"

"Ko wanted to save the most important items! She is the courageous one!"

Indeed, Ko had been the hero. She had gone through so much for Mother and me when we fled Nanam. Now this!

Hideyo said he had walked all the way back from the hospital as fast as he could. He must have been exhausted. I did not tell him how scared and mad I was while he was gone.

"Little One, get me some cash," Hideyo ordered. "I must pay the doctor. We still have lots to do tonight." Hideyo untied the damp wrapping-cloth bundle, and I pulled everything out onto the ground. In the secret pocket of the wrapping cloth was the cash Mother had brought from our house in the bamboo grove. Ko said it was emergency money. She never wanted to touch this hidden cash.

As Hideyo left for the doctor's office, he told me to start packing to move.

MOVING

When Hideyo returned he had a few groceries: rice, miso, and one stalk of green onion. He said, "We will cook our supper at the hospital so that Ko can eat." I told him I wanted to go after the daikon greens. But first I had to find my shoes.

The smell of smoke permeated the warehouse. The concrete floor was flooded with water. The stairway had completely fallen down. I looked up to see the four-tatami-mat room where we had lived. There was a burned hole, and brown water dripped down to where I stood. One tatami mat was hanging from a wall post. I searched for my faded red leather shoes. Hoping nothing would fall on me, I carefully moved piles of burned scraps. The two old cooking pots from Mrs. Masuda, chopsticks, and our three wooden soup bowls were floating on the water. Ko's black shoes, unharmed but wet, were scattered by the front door. I spotted the soaked apple box, upside down—the box where we ate and studied, the box we used as a cupboard for the eating utensils and as an altar for Mother's urn and the sword. I picked it up like it was a dear old friend. My heart almost stopped when I spotted my burned red shoes nestled behind the fallen stairway. I picked them up. They were discolored and shriveled from the fire. "My shoes are dead!" I cried. They had been part of me; they had journeyed with me all the way from Nanam, Korea, to Kyoto, Japan.

I put Ko's and my shoes, the cooking pots, soup bowls, and chopsticks into the apple box. Before returning to the stream bank, I went across the streetcar tracks to see Mr. and Mrs. Masuda. There were pieces of white substance scattered over the streetcar rails and on the road. I took a closer look: my daikons! Some had been smashed and broken into pieces by passing streetcars, and some had been stepped on. I felt terribly ashamed of my angry thought that the policeman had stolen my vegetables. I picked up the big pieces and put them into the apple box.

As I came near I clearly saw that the Masudas' house was roped off and that two policemen, including the one who had helped me, were standing outside. I greeted my policeman politely, for I felt guilty about doubting him. I told him about Ko. He wished for Ko's speedy recovery and said he felt badly that he had not been able to find my shoes. He said the police chief had assigned him to guard the Masudas' house and he did not have time to look. "No need." I shook my head and showed him my ruined pair. He felt terrible for me.

"I wanted to see the Masudas before we go. I have not seen them for quite a while," I said, beginning to duck under the rope.

"Ah! You do not know," said the policeman sympathetically. "Both of them were burned to death in the factory. Their niece is coming to take care of things."

I stared at the policeman. I could not utter a word. My blood rushed from my head. Now I realized who the men in white coats were: the coroner and his assistant. What had Mr. and Mrs. Masuda been doing in the factory at such a late hour? I never saw them work after 6 P.M. I remembered the gentle way Mrs. Masuda came to help Ko and me when Mother died. She protected us. She was happy with the way we kept the warehouse, loaned us her old cooking pots, and told us to ask her for whatever we needed.

Carrying the apple box that held all the things I had picked up from the flooded warehouse and the pieces of daikon, I ran all the way back to where Hideyo was packing our belongings. Sniffling, I told him the bad news of the Masudas and showed him what I had found in the warehouse.

"I just heard it at the doctor's office," Brother said with sorrow. "They were a sincere couple. It's too bad!"

"My precious shoes are dead, too!" I cried, and showed him the discolored, hardened, and shriveled pair. Now the toes were burst open like angry animals' mouths.

Hideyo extended his hands as if to say, Give me the shoes. I put them in his hands. Hideyo gazed at me and the shoes for a long time. He bit his lower lip and took a big sigh to control his emotions.

"Now, about your shoes. We must treat them respectfully," he said as if he were the funeral-parlor man. "Let us have a burial at the stream!"

"You mean you are going to dump my shoes in the stream?" I sniffled.

"No. Not dump. Float," said Hideyo. "Would you like to do it? I will say prayers."

"I cannot do it!" I cried.

Hideyo then knelt down by the stream, gently placed the pair on the water, and said, "You served my little sister well. She thanks you, and I thank you. Now float down the stream . . . to a big river . . . to the ocean . . . float to the river behind the bamboo grove where we swam. Carry our message to Father. Say Ko is very ill, and hurry home. We need him. . . ." Hideyo's voice trembled and he could not say more. He wiped his tears.

The shoes separated in the current, tumbling as they went down the stream. I cried and watched until they were seen no more. I did not want to leave.

Hideyo gently patted my back. "Remember what Father told us. 'You must not cry or fuss over what you've lost. You must appreciate what you still have.' I will make you a pair of clogs as soon as we settle. Now let us move on."

"I wish we could stay in Mrs. Masuda's shed," I said, wiping the tears on my sleeves.

"We cannot, Little One." Hideyo shook his head.

"Where are we going to live? Back at the station?" Hideyo did not answer. His eyes were filled with tears, so I lost the courage to ask more questions.

Then he said the doctor had given him permission to leave our belongings in his shed until we could settle ourselves. "Ready, Little One?" he asked.

Hideyo put Ko's and my stuffed rucksacks onto my back. He hung the canteens, two of them still filled with water, around my neck. He asked if I was strong enough to carry the bucket. In the bucket he'd put the old cooking pots, the chopsticks, the wooden soup bowls, and the daikon pieces. I said I was strong enough. Thinking of Ko's suffering, I was not about to admit how tired I was. Hideyo told me to go, leave everything at the shed, and come back.

"Ask the doctor to loan us some ropes so that I can bundle all our bedding," he said.

Because the two rucksacks were heavy, I leaned forward as I walked. Every time I made a step, five canteens bumped my knees. I was glad they were not all filled with water. I had to change the hand that held the bucket many times. The load on my back felt like a thousand tons. I thought I would never reach the doctor's shed. When I finally arrived, I took a big sigh of relief and rested a few moments before I opened the doctor's door.

I called timidly, "Good evening." Though Mrs. Yamada and I had never met, she knew who I was. I bowed deeply.

"I have already opened the shed door for you. It is dark there. Take this," she said, handing me a flashlight and showing me how to turn on the switch. The light hit my trousers. "My! You are wet!" she exclaimed. Her eyes moved up and down. "Barefoot, too!"

I told her how everything we owned was damp and that my only shoes were burned up.

"While you are at the shed, I will look for my old clothes," she said, and pointed at her clogs. "In the meantime, wear these."

The shed was about ten steps away from the house. It smelled like rubbing alcohol. I flashed the light here and there to see where I could put our things. There were lots of cardboard boxes of all sizes neatly stacked deep in the shed. I read

some of the signs on the boxes. GAUZE, BAN-
DAGES, OXYGENATED WATER, INJECTION SYRINGE. I
arranged our possessions near the door. The
warmth in the shed made me sleepy. I wished
Hideyo and I could make our home here.

Mrs. Yamada prepared tea and waited on me.
The hot tea tasted delicious. While I was sipping,
Mrs. Yamada spread out her old clothes. "Try
these now, before you catch pneumonia," she
said. I was hesitant to change, for fear Dr.
Yamada would come, but Mrs. Yamada pulled
down my wet trousers and spotted the blisters
on my legs. "You were burned!" she shouted,
and called for her husband.

"What is happening?" questioned the doctor
calmly in a deep, low voice.

"It is absolutely *nothing*," I said, quickly putting
on Mrs. Yamada's old trousers and bowing deeply
to the doctor. Though she said they were too small
for her, I swam in her baggy pants.

"Both her legs are covered with blisters!" said
Mrs. Yamada.

"Let me see," ordered the doctor. I did not
want him to, because I had no money to pay for
an examination.

"I am all right," I said as I folded my own wet
trousers.

"Let me see," the doctor insisted. He ordered
Mrs. Yamada to get an ointment jar from his
office and smeared greasy medicine on my legs.

Dry clothes and hot tea made me relax. The

doctor asked me question after question about our escape from Nanam. But I could not stay there any longer, knowing Hideyo was waiting for me on the stream bank. I told the doctor I would come back again to tell him more stories.

Mrs. Yamada asked if I would care to have another cup of tea. "Yes, please," I said, thinking I could bring it to Ko in my empty canteen. Mrs. Yamada reached out for my teacup. "I will go get my canteen from the shed. It will be for my sister," I said.

Mrs. Yamada said she would fill the canteen while I went to the stream for another load. I asked the doctor how much the examination would cost. As he handed me a small jar full of ointment and a rope for Hideyo, he said I'd paid the fee by telling him the exciting story of our escape.

I rushed back to Hideyo with the rope. Hideyo was glad to see me in dry clothes. "You look so grown-up in those!" he said. While I was gone Hideyo had gathered more wooden scraps and packed them neatly in the apple box. He wrapped the box in a blanket and he put it on my back, tying it securely with a piece of rope. He made a huge bundle of our futons and the wrapping-cloth bundle and then tied them together tightly. He squatted on the ground, his back facing the bedding, and pulled his arms through the rope. Hideyo said, "When I shout 'three,' you must lift the end of the futon to help me stand." The load was extremely heavy.

"Honorable Brother, why don't we make two trips to the shed? Your load is too heavy!" I said, knowing he was exhausted.

"Let's go, Little One! We have no time to waste," he said, ignoring my suggestion. "We *must* go forward . . . keep on forward!" He sounded as though he were whipping himself to go forward with his own words.

As I walked slowly along in the clogs, the glow of sunset tinted the earth and the stream. I envied the crows that cawed as they flew above my head: They were going home to sleep.

After leaving our loads at the shed, we took two blankets and the rope with us to the old man's small vegetable field. The dark enveloped us completely, but it was not hard to find the piles of daikon greens. Hideyo and I packed the greens in the blankets. We each carried a bundle. I said to Hideyo that I wished I had brought a sheet of paper and a pencil to leave a note of thanks for the old man. Hideyo said, "When Ko's condition is settled, we will both come here to thank him in person." We were tired and hungry. Not talking, we plodded on.

Hideyo broke the silence. "We will take what's absolutely necessary to the hospital tonight. There is not enough room for everything."

"Will they let us both stay there?" I asked, worrying about where we would sleep.

"The hospital said they can hire a private nurse for Ko, or we can nurse her ourselves. We cannot afford a nursing person. If you look after Ko, I can go to work," Hideyo said.

"You mean I do not have to go to school?" I whooped for joy. Since school had not been a happy place for me, I would much rather stay with Ko.

"I must earn," said Hideyo. "I am sorry you have to miss your schooling for a while, but you can catch up. I know you can!"

We walked back to the Yamadas'. With the help of the flashlight, Hideyo rearranged our humble possessions in the shed. He put Ko's and my beddings plus the wrapping-cloth bundle on his back. I carried the apple box filled with wood scraps that was wrapped in Hideyo's blanket. I also took the canteens, some daikon greens, and household items in the water bucket.

"Ko must be very hungry," Hideyo said. "Let us take a streetcar tonight."

"Do you have enough money for that?" I asked.

He nodded and said, "The doctor did not charge me, except for the taxi fare."

The streetcar was almost empty. We dropped our bundles onto the seats. I leaned on the apple box, rested my head, and soon went to sleep.

"Wake up! Little One!" Hideyo said, shaking me gently. "We are there."

Though I was terribly sleepy, the thought of seeing Ko brought me quickly awake.

IN THE HOSPITAL

Ko was lying on an iron cot on a bare tatami mat. Both her legs and her right arm were in casts. Her chest and abdomen were covered with a small hospital blanket. The room was dimly lit and slightly larger than our room in the warehouse. Ko's clothes hung on one of three long nails on the wall.

I dropped my bundles on the floor. "Honorable Sister! I am here!" I called. Seeing my big sister lying motionless made me choke with tears.

She opened her badly bruised, swollen eyes, and turned her head slightly toward me. She smiled, and said something I could not hear. I brought my good ear to her lips. "Where is Brother?" she asked. I told her he'd gone to the nurses' station.

"I bet you are hungry," I said, trying hard not to cry. "I will cook something good for you now. I also have a surprise!" I hung the tea canteen on the wall next to Ko's clothes.

Hideyo bumped his huge bundle on the sliding glass door as he came in. "We must make a bed for Ko immediately," he said. He pushed the iron cot away from the wall and told me to go between the wall and the cot. Standing on the opposite side of the cot, he said, "When I tilt Ko toward me, you must slide the futon under her." After

43

we'd done that, Hideyo and I switched positions. He tilted Ko again. She gritted her teeth and I was able to spread the futon completely under her.

When she was covered with the futon comforter Ko said, "Thanks. I was cold."

I needed some water to start our supper. Hideyo told me there was a huge wooden sink in the corner at the end of the very dark hallway. Small pieces of fish bone were scattered in the sink. I figured it was the place where people washed food, eating utensils, and even hand laundry.

When I returned with a bucket full of water, Hideyo was opening the sliding window. Attached to the windowsill was a small board, slightly larger than a snack table. Much to my surprise, there was an old *shichirin*, like a hibachi, probably used for cooking. Hideyo put some crumpled magazine papers into the shichirin. He shaved pieces of scrap wood and then went to the nurses' station to borrow a tiny box of matches. He heated water in the bucket. As soon as it was hot enough, he poured the water into the empty canteens to make hot-water bottles. He wrapped them in our undershirts and put them by Ko's feet.

I cooked a cup of rice in a smaller pot, then set it aside. While I made miso soup, adding thinly sliced daikon and finely chopped green onion, Hideyo arranged the remaining daikon greens, the apple box filled with wood scraps, and the wrapping-cloth bundle under Ko's bed. I mixed cooked rice and miso soup in Ko's small wooden soup bowl.

"Honorable Sister! Supper time! We are going to have rice!" I called excitedly and cheerfully. "Open your mouth." But there was no spoon and I could not feed her soupy rice with chopsticks. The best I could do was to put five to six grains of rice at a time in Ko's mouth. "I wish I had a spoon," I grumbled.

Hideyo was sitting on the floor eating a small portion of rice and sipping soup. He asked how Ko was doing.

I told him, "Our sister would be eating so much better if I had a spoon."

"Little One! Why don't you use your head!" said Hideyo, grinning as he stood. He reached for the tea canteen, unscrewed the cap, and dipped it into the soup bowl. He scooped up soupy rice and acted as if he were feeding a baby, saying, "Now, open your mouth . . . wide . . . wide . . . and wide!

"See? Isn't this a good idea?" he said, showing me his mischievous smile. "Where is your head? A head is to *think*, Little One! Not just for growing hair!" I burst out laughing at Hideyo borrowing Father's words. Ko laughed weakly.

As I ate, I wondered if the day would ever come when we could be seated all together with Father, eating a very fresh, sliced raw-fish dish called sashimi, sushi, and even sukiyaki until we were stuffed.

When Ko was finished, Hideyo handed me the empty bowl.

"Now, I have a surprise." I grinned.

"Surprise?" questioned Hideyo. "What is it?"

I rinsed Ko's bowl and poured some tea. The green tea was lukewarm now, but just right for my sister to drink. When Hideyo saw Ko's uninjured hand was weak and shaking, he lifted her head slightly to let her sip comfortably. Tears streamed from Ko's black, swollen eyes.

"Where did you get tea?" asked Hideyo.

"I am a magician!" I smiled. As I served some for Hideyo, I said, "It was from Mrs. Yamada." While I watched them drink tea, I couldn't help thinking about our escape from the bamboo grove. We were fleeing on the hospital train. Smoke was everywhere, and I fainted. When I came to, Ko gave me a caramel to suck on to soothe my throat. When I asked her where she'd gotten it, Ko said, "I am a magician!"

I stored the leftover rice and miso soup in my mess kit. Ko would need food to get well fast. I filled the tea canteen, now empty, with hot water and put it on Ko's abdomen. Before I spread my futon under Ko's bed, I wrote on a postcard, in my smallest print, to Corporal Matsumura in Morioka, telling him of Ko's mishap and the hospital address. The corporal was the family friend who had urged us to escape from Nanam, then found Ko and me in Kyoto after reading my essay in the national newspaper. Whenever he could, he sent us dried seafood, leftover material, thread, and notes of encouragement saying, "Keep on! Honorable Father will return!"

Because Hideyo did not bring his own futon, I made him a bed with my futon comforter on the small floor space next to the wall. I spread my futon under Ko's cot. Happy to have a safe place to sleep, I huddled near the wrapping-cloth bundle that now held Mother's ashes and the sword, and then covered myself with a small hospital blanket. The smell of fresh daikon greens mixed strongly with the smell of the smoky pillow I made from Ko's clothes. When I stretched, hairy greens tickled my foot. Somewhere on my way to slumber land, I heard Hideyo chipping a piece of wood.

I was wakened by the sound of the door sliding open. It was my habit to sleep with my good ear up so that I could hear things. Someone entered the room stealthily. A flashlight spotted here and there. I was not fully awake yet, and I did not know where I was. When I tried to sit up, my head bumped on the iron cot, and I realized I was under Ko's bed in the hospital. Then the footsteps went toward Hideyo. The light flashed on him for a few moments. I thought, A doctor who wanted to check Ko would come straight to her bed, and a nurse would come with him. I curled myself tightly and kept still. Now, silent footsteps came toward Ko's bed. The flashlight beamed down and I saw hairy legs and big bare feet in front of my eyes. A robber!

The robber flashed the light on Ko, and forcefully put his hand between her futon mattress and the cot to look for something—maybe a purse or jewels. If he did not find what he wanted, he would threaten and maybe kill Ko!

My heart drummed wildly. I must get the sword and slash his legs to pieces! In a curled-up position, I reached for the wrapping-cloth bundle. But I could not untie the knot. Why did Hideyo keep tying it so tightly? I was irritated. I wanted to get Hideyo's attention by calling him but something told me to stay quiet. Why had Hideyo not wakened? Surely he must have heard someone coming in. He had perfect hearing! I quietly shifted my position so that I could crawl out to grab the robber's legs, but while I was turning, my hands touched the daikon greens. I grabbed as many as I could hold and scooted out to rub the prickly greens fiercely all over the robber's feet and legs.

"A ghost!" he screamed. "A ghost!" The robber dropped the flashlight and quickly ran to the door. But his way was blocked by Hideyo.

I leaped out of my bed. Hideyo yelled for the nurses and I searched for the string that hung from the ceiling to turn on the light. The robber, much taller than Hideyo, was wearing a winter army-uniform top and trousers shredded below his knees. He held a knife up high and was about to attack Hideyo! Hideyo caught the robber's wrist and twisted it until the robber dropped the knife. I picked the knife up, but my hands were shaky. The robber had gotten into the corridor and was struggling to get away from Hideyo. Their bodies banged the doors and walls. Hearing such a loud commotion, neighboring patients who were able to walk gathered about. The robber freed his left hand and tried to hit Hideyo's head. But Hideyo, using a judo technique, entwined his right leg with the robber's and knocked him flat on the floor with a great thud.

"Rope! Rope, Little One!" Hideyo hollered. He pinned the robber down with his weight and held the robber's hands tightly behind his back. "Tie his hands!" Hideyo commanded.

Three nurses came running to the scene. They helped us put the rope around the robber's hands and legs. The robber squirmed. The nurses' hands and mine were trembling, but we managed. One nurse ran to call the police.

Neighboring patients, curious yet frightened, looked down at the robber. A male patient shouted, "Well done!" Another exclaimed, "Good! Beat him up! I bet he stole all my money last week. Give it back! Give it back!"

Two policemen arrived. They handcuffed the robber and untied the rope.

"The robbers always go for the patients' beds. They think it is where a purse or money is hidden," said one policeman to the onlookers. "Often they strike the patients with dangerous tools. Beware!"

I gave the policeman the robber's knife and flashlight. He copied our names and they took the robber away.

A doctor hastened into Ko's room. He examined her to be sure the robber had not harmed her. He gave her a shot, saying it would ease the pain and help her to relax. Everything quieted down once more. I was about to crawl under the cot to sleep, but seeing Hideyo straightening out the rope made me uneasy. More robbers might come, again and again, to attack Ko.

"I am scared. Please, Honorable Brother, untie the wrapping cloth so that I can get to the sword easily."

"There is nothing to be scared of. The sword must not be seen by anyone. We must protect it," Hideyo said. Then he asked, "Little One, what did you do to frighten the robber?"

"I rubbed his legs with the daikon greens." Remembering how irritated I was with Hideyo, I asked why he had not gotten up right away when the robber entered. Was he asleep?

"I was awake."

"Then why didn't you get him immediately? I was trembling!"

"Because I saw him pull out a knife by Ko's bed. If I jumped on him then, he might have harmed our sister. While he was searching for money, I crawled to the door and waited. You did well, Little One. Now let's get some sleep. I am exhausted." Hideyo yawned.

Ko had been listening quietly.

"Honorable Sister, how could you keep still? Weren't you frightened?" I asked.

"Sure I was," said Ko in a weak tone. "Thoughts went through my mind. If I were killed, how would you two manage without me? Another thought was, I will be with Mother forever!"

"It's not *time* for you to leave Little One and me," said Hideyo. "Each one of us has a purpose on this earth. We were put here to develop ourselves. Now, let's all sleep!"

"Can we keep the light on?" I asked. "I am really scared."

"Baby!" Hideyo laughed, but he left the light on and covered his eyes with a thin washcloth.

Though I crawled back under Ko's bed to sleep, the incident kept me awake. I heard Ko's head turning right to left and left to right many times. I crawled out and took a peek.

Because her eyes were swollen, I wondered how well she could see things. I put my face very near to hers. "Are you warm enough?" I whispered. She nodded, but each time she tried to move her body to be comfortable, she moaned. "You are in pain," I said, wanting to do something to ease her hurt. "Shall I give you water to drink?" She shook her head and whispered, "I can stand this excruciating pain. The worst pain

I am having now is thinking about how I am going to pay the mountainous medical bill."

Because I did not want to disturb Hideyo's sleep, I whispered, "There is the wrapping-cloth money."

"That is not enough!" Ko gave a big sigh. "Everything is inflated now."

I said, "I will sell your wares from sunup to sundown. At night, I will learn to sew well. I will make more beanbags, or even aprons for housewives."

Hideyo sat up. "Gosh, Little Sisters!" he grumbled. "Your whispering makes more noise than if you were talking out loud. We all should be sleeping. I have not had decent sleep for the past two nights."

"I thought you were asleep," I said in my normal voice. "Sister cannot sleep. She is worrying about how to pay the medical bills."

"Don't you know it doesn't do any good to worry yourself sick about anything now? There is nothing we can do at this *moment*. Why not relax and have a good sleep?"

"I will crawl under the bed and behave if you go with me to the toilet," I said.

"You can go yourself," Hideyo said.

I told him I was not brave after what had happened.

"Come!" Hideyo stood.

All along the dimly lit corridor I heard the patients' low moans and groans. Even my own shadow looked as if someone were about to jump on me from the rear. Everything seemed eerie.

I asked Hideyo to wait for me. "You can get back yourself," he said. "I am going to the nurses' station to borrow a bedpan for Ko." I ran on tiptoe all the way back to Ko's room. When I crawled onto my futon, my heart was thumping louder than ever.

MORNING

When I crept out from under Ko's bed, the sun was streaming onto the floor through the small windowpanes. Hideyo had already gone to work. He'd left a note: "Little One. I made a wooden spoon for you so you can feed Ko. Use the shavings to build a fire. The match is beneath the comforter where I slept. It was a good bed you made. Roll it up, will you? Be sure to keep Ko warm. Thanks."

Very silently I took a paper-thin washcloth and a toothbrush with its almost flat bristles from my rucksack. I did not have any toothpaste. I took Mrs. Masuda's large cooking pot to use as a washbasin. I stepped out to the corridor and closed the door soundlessly.

There were several men and women with their buckets, teakettles, or washbasins and towels standing in lines to get some water from the faucets. They were talking about last night's robber. A woman washing clothes in the huge wooden sink stopped what she was doing and listened. A man next to her with toothpaste all around his mouth quickly rinsed it and said he saw a young man, a tiny girl, and a nurse courageously roping the robber. "If I were well enough, I would have helped the young man!" he added.

A short, thin woman in a yellow kimono bed gown, her long black hair loosely bound at her back, stood in front of me, holding an aluminum teakettle. She turned to me and said she had not heard the commotion last night. "Did you?" she asked. I told her it happened in our room, and it was my brother who caught the robber. "Hero!" she praised. She was pale and looked as though it was a chore for her to stand. There were many beads of sweat on her wide forehead.

We exchanged names. She was Mrs. Minato and she had been in the hospital for two weeks. Her room was three doors down from where we were. When Mrs. Minato's turn came, she filled her teakettle, but she was not strong enough to hold it. She staggered, and grabbed my right arm and I swayed, too, but I braced myself to protect her from falling.

"I thought," she panted, "I was brave enough to make myself a cup of tea."

I told her, "I will bring your teakettle as soon as I wash myself." Leaning her back against the corridor wall, she slowly walked sideways to her room.

I drew some cold water into the cooking pot and washed myself. A chill went through me, tightening every muscle in my body. My thoughts flew to Father in Manchuria, where a severe winter comes quickly.

Mrs. Minato was resting on her bed, breathing heavily, but she gave me a weak smile. She asked if I would put the teakettle on the shichirin by the window. "I will build a fire later on," she said. She told me there were a few pieces of cake in her cupboard. She wanted me to take a piece.

"A cake!" I almost shouted. I hadn't eaten a piece of cake in two years, since we left Nanam. My mouth was already watering. Mrs. Minato handed me a tissue paper to wrap it in.

Holding the piece of yellow cake with creamy icing very carefully, I tiptoed into Ko's room. She was still asleep. I hid the cake under Ko's bed. It would surprise and cheer her. It would make Ko well fast! Silently I opened the window halfway. The wind was blowing away from our room. It was safe to start a fire. I reheated the canteen hot-water bottles, rewrapped them in our underwear, and put them back by Ko's feet and stomach.

I boiled hot water in a small pot and drank it. I thought of Mrs. Minato, who wanted to have a cup of tea, and decided to bring her a pot full of hot water. Before I went to Mrs. Minato's, I put the bucket, half filled with water, on the shichirin, figuring, There will be enough hot water to wash Ko when I return.

Mrs. Minato was glad of the unexpected treat, and told me her tea and food supplies were also in the cupboard. Watching her sip the tea, I asked if she had someone to look after her. She said her mother had been staying with her but caught a cold and had gone home yesterday.

"It is hard for my mother to look after me," Mrs. Minato said. "She is eighty years old."

I envied Mrs. Minato. I thought to myself, how lucky she is to have a mother still, even if she is eighty! At the same time, waves of sadness surged over me and I almost shed tears for my missing mother. At times like these we all need our mothers. Only Mother could give Ko gentle care. Listening to Mother's singing or stories would cure Ko quickly.

I did not want Mrs. Minato to see my tear-filled eyes, so I turned my head away from her to look at the sky. I swallowed some lumps and forced myself to be cheerful. "It's going to be a nice day."

"Why are you in the hospital?" she asked. "You look healthy enough."

I told her, "I am nursing my big sister, who is suffering from broken bones."

"Where are your parents?" she asked.

I burst out crying and told her, "We are refugees, and Mother is dead. We do not know where Father is. But we have a big brother," I added proudly, trying to get away from this sad conversation.

I quickly poured the remaining hot water into Mrs. Minato's washbasin, thinking, She can wash her face with it. As I turned to go back to Ko's room, Mrs. Minato stopped me. She said she could not eat all the cake. Would I take two more pieces, one for my sister and one for my brother?

"A whole piece of cake for each of us!" I exclaimed. I bowed deeply, with a great big smile for her generosity. Holding the extra cakes carefully in the empty cooking pot, I went back to Ko's room. I hid the two pieces of cake next to the first one.

Ko was still asleep. I put my good ear closer to see if she was breathing. The water in the bucket was simmering. Moving it from the fire, I heated last night's leftover miso soup in Ko's mess kit, adding more water and chopped daikon greens to make it go further. While the soup was cooking slowly, I rolled the comforter that Hideyo had slept on and pushed it into the corner.

A nurse came to check on Ko. I told her that my sister had been sleeping for a long time and asked if I should wake her for breakfast. The nurse said, "Let her sleep. She needs it."

Then she added, "Every nursing person must tidy up the patient's room and mop a part of the hallway floor. The patient's door must stay open during the day so that the doctor can enter easily." I told her I had no cleaning equipment. She said there were lots of rags and cleaning supplies in the hallway closet. "Help yourself," she added before she went on to the next patient.

The closet was dark, but when my eyes gradually got used to it, I saw that a string hung from the ceiling. A used eraser was tied to the end of the string. I pulled it to turn on the light.

The closet was as large as Ko's room. On the left side, scattered on the floor, were several pieces of cotton kimono-style bed gowns. Some people must have discarded their bedclothes when they were released. I took the first piece. It was very stiff. I brought it near the light to take a good look. At one glance I tossed it back in fright. It was a piece of bloodstained gown. I came across a man's kimono, lined with gauze. This will be very nice for Ko! I thought. Then I saw a gown patterned with morning glories. Its sleeves were cut off. Someone must have used the sleeves for dust cloths. The kimono smelled musty. If I washed it, I could make dish towels. I'd use the small pieces of cloth for rags.

I drew some water into a hospital bucket, wet a rag, and pushed it along the hallway floor on all fours. It did not take me long to finish Ko's room. The water in the bucket wasn't too dirty, and Ko was still asleep. I hastened to Mrs. Minato's hallway floor to do her portion. Her door was wide open and she waved at me to enter. "How good of you," she said. I told her I would do a quick job of tidying her room also. "Would you?" she asked. I nodded and kept on working, because I did not want to take the time to talk to her. I did not know just when Ko would wake up and look for me.

As soon as I got back to Ko's, a slender-faced middle-aged man in a white hospital gown came in, followed by a nurse. "I am Professor Akanuma. A surgeon," he introduced himself.

"I am the patient's sister. Good morning, sir," I replied with a bow. The surgeon uncovered naked Ko and she woke up. The nurse was standing by the surgeon with a clipboard, so I went around and stood by Ko's head. I wanted to see the surgeon examine her. He picked up the canteen hot-water bottles and asked, "What are these?"

"Canteens, sir. To keep my sister warm," I answered. The surgeon grinned.

Ko's eyes searched for me. "Why aren't you in school today?" she asked in her still-sleepy, weak voice.

"I have to nurse you, Honorable Sister," I whispered. In spite of everything, I was glad I did not have to go to school.

The surgeon examined Ko. She was terribly swollen. Her right foot was especially bad and it was very purple. He tapped her right toes and asked Ko if she felt hurt or numb. "Numb," said my sister. He took Ko's pulse and nodded to himself as if satisfied. He checked Ko's medical chart with the nurse. Again he nodded.

"Do you have a bed gown for her?" he asked me.

I said, "Yes, but it needs washing."

"Keep your sister warm. She can stand more

canteens!" he said, going off to see the next patient.

When the surgeon was out of Ko's sight, she asked, "Why didn't you go to school?" Her voice sounded shaken but angry. She noticed my clothes. "Where did you get them?"

I cheerfully explained Mrs. Yamada's kindness so that Ko would be in a good mood. Then I said gently, "I cannot leave you alone. You need my help." I was feeling delighted about missing school, but also proud that my big sister needed me.

"No, I do not. I can take care myself!" Ko snapped.

"What?" I matched her snapping. "How? You cannot even feed yourself."

"Watch me," said Ko. "Put a piece of daikon on my chest."

"Daikon is easy to eat," I said. All she had to do was to pick it up in her left hand and put it in her mouth. Challenging her, I half filled her soup bowl with watery soup and carefully put it on her chest. Ko picked it up with her good hand and, raising her head a little, slowly sipped the soup without wasting a drop. She dropped her head down with a big sigh.

I marveled at Ko's determination. "Would you care to have a second bowl?" I asked. She said, "A little more, but give me a few moments to catch my breath."

"You are still weak. You cannot do everything. You need me," I told her.

"There is nothing I cannot do," said Ko. Her

voice was weak, but in each word I read her willfulness.

"Then how are you going to manage the toilet?" I asked. "The nurses are not going to help you. They are busy with terminal patients."

"You will help me with the bedpan before you go to school. I will be all right until you come back."

"I cannot think about school. I want to help Mrs. Minato until her mother returns."

"Hideyo has been working hard to make monthly school tuition payments for you," said Ko. "Don't you dare waste his money!" I had heard the same words so many times that I felt like screaming. She did not know what I went through at school. But today I stayed silent. She has gone through enough, I thought.

"What time is it?" asked Ko. I hastened to the nurses' station to take a peek at the clock. It was half past eleven. Ko said I could still make it to the afternoon class. I said that all my schoolbooks were in Dr. Yamada's shed.

"Dr. Yamada's shed? Why?" questioned Ko. I told her what had happened since her accident, and that Mr. and Mrs. Masuda had burned to death in the fire. Her swollen, blackened eyes stared at me for a few moments as if she could not believe me.

"Ah! . . . No! No!" sighed Ko. "What were they doing in the factory at that hour?" She stared at the stained ceiling for a long time, and then gave another heavy sigh. Abruptly she said, "Well, you go on and get your school things now." I told her it would take me all afternoon and part of the evening to walk there and back.

"Where is my blouse? There should be some change in the pocket. Take a streetcar."

"I still cannot go." I told her about finding the kimonos in the hallway closet. I showed them to her. "I want to boil the bed gown so that you can wear it," I said.

"They are such big pieces that you need a washtub," said Ko. "Since we do not have one, wash them in the stream behind the warehouse. While they are drying on the pebbly bank, go to the doctor's shed to get all your school things. After that you must go to the Masudas' house and express our condolences to their niece, Junko."

I did not mind going all that way to the stream to wash clothes, but to face the burned warehouse would hurt me. Also, I knew how painful it must be for Junko to lose both aunt and uncle at the same time. For Ko and me Mrs. Masuda had been like an "aunty." I would burst into tears and wouldn't be able to utter a word to express our sympathy. Then, too, picking up my schoolbooks meant I must continue my schooling. The thought of going back to the school made me feel worse. In all, I thought it would be much nicer if I did not have to make the trip to our old home. I gave Ko another bowl of watery soup. Watching her drink it, I thought, Persuade her by keeping very busy.

"I will give you a sponge bath," I said, adding wood scraps to the shichirin to make the fire strong.

Ko paid no attention. She asked, "How many abandoned kimonos were there in the closet?"

"Several," I told her.

"Go get all of them."

"All of them? What are you going to do with them?"

"You are always asking, why, how, and what," said Ko disgustedly. "Do as I say. Don't ask so many questions."

"I do not want to touch the bloody one," I said to her. "Every time I see bloodstained things, my memory goes back to our frightful escape. I just cannot get over it."

"Who can? Our mental wounds will never heal. You have to learn to develop inner strength. Go! Get the rest of the kimonos and show them to me."

I reluctantly went to the closet, thinking, Ko is an invalid now, and still she tells me what to do! I could have spanked myself for telling her about the bloody kimono. Ko would never have known about it if I had kept my mouth shut.

I showed each kimono to Ko. I watched her expression as I spread the bloody one. Her black, swollen eyes were motionless. Remembering last night and the robber's knife made me imagine that the man who wore this kimono was murdered in his bed. I felt sick.

"I can use them all," said Ko. "I will make you nice clothes as soon as I am able to sit up. For the time being, fold and store them under your futon."

"Water is boiling now. It's time for a bath," I said.

"After supper," she answered. Once Ko made up her mind, she would never change it. I put out the fire by pouring some water over the shichirin. I stowed the man's kimono lined with gauze and the morning-glory cloth in Ko's rucksack. As I stepped out to close the door behind me, I heard Ko's weak call: "Be careful!"

BLAMED

The streetcar stopped near the Masudas'. Where the factory once stood was now open space, and the wind blew hard from the field. I did not know until then how much I missed the land around the old warehouse. I went straight to the stream, glad no one was nearby. My laundry-pounding stick was still there, as if it were waiting for me. Standing in the water, I wet the man's bedclothes and the morning-glory cloth and lay them on the flat rock. I beat them extra hard to kill all the germs. The wet items were extremely heavy, so I had a hard time wringing them out. I spread them on the pebbly bank and put large rocks on the corners.

I walked toward Dr. Yamada's house, carrying the empty rucksack. His office faced the streetcar tracks. Behind his office a short roofed corridor stretched to his residence. Just as I was turning to go to his house to let Mrs. Yamada know I was there, a short, stout man came out of the doctor's office. His neck was wrapped with a white bandage. He turned his back to me and walked away slowly.

That back! I had seen the very same back between the warehouse and the clog factory the night of the fire. I followed the man. He turned right on a narrow, winding dirt road where the houses stood in a row. At almost the end of the road he made another right turn, and I lost him. There were shacks, like tenement houses, piled together in this area. In front of these houses ran an uncovered sewer. Often children as well as men used the gutter for a toilet. The whole area smelled.

I went back to the doctor's house and asked Mrs. Yamada for a key to the shed. All my school supplies, Ko's sewing box, and her handicrafts fit into the rucksack. On my way to return the key to Mrs. Yamada, I met the doctor in the corridor. He was happy to see me and wanted to examine my blisters. "Besides, it's teatime," he announced.

"How is your big sister?" the doctor asked. I

told him and his wife about Ko's condition and how Hideyo and I were looking after her and about our hot-water-bottle canteens. I ended my talk by telling how Hideyo caught the robber. They listened with glee, and the doctor ordered his wife to get a hot-water bottle and bedpan from the office to loan to us.

When she left, I told the doctor I'd seen a short, stout man with bandages around his neck leaving his office about twenty minutes earlier. "Who was he, and what happened to his neck?"

"He is Goro," the doctor said. "Goro told me he was watching the factory fire and some hot object flew onto his neck. Why?"

"Two evenings ago he was walking around the factory. I greeted him, but he did not answer. That's why." I used the word *greet* because I wanted the doctor to feel it was my casual evening greeting to a passerby. I did not tell him about Goro's suspicious actions around the factory at dusk and about Ko's fire stick. I wanted to be sure he was the one who had hidden in the outhouse before making an accusation.

"I think he worked at the factory," said the doctor.

Mrs. Yamada returned with a hot-water bottle and a bedpan. I stowed them in the rucksack. Their wall clock already pointed to 3:30 P.M.

I went next to the Masudas' house. Because the conversation with the doctor and his wife had been so pleasant, I thought I would be able to express our condolences to Junko without difficulty.

"*Konnichiwa*! Good afternoon," I called loudly at the entrance as I opened the door.

A woman of about thirty-five appeared. "Yes? I am Junko Masuda. What can I do for you?" Bowing deeply to her, I introduced myself. She gave me a nasty stare. As I was about to express our sympathy, she screamed, "You! You are the one who set fire to the factory. You killed my uncle and aunt! Where is their cash box? Your sister stole their money!"

Shocked, I shouted, "We did not!"

"Shut up! I already reported you to the police!" She screamed, "Bring the cash box back! If you don't, I will turn you over to the authorities!" Before I could say that we were innocent, she grabbed my right shoulder and threw me out into the street. I lost my balance and fell sideways on the pavement.

The streetcar rushed past at great speed, spraying sparks.

"Too bad you were not run over! Thief!" Junko Masuda roughly slammed the entrance door. I got up and ran at the door. I wanted to tell her I knew nothing of the cash box and did not set the fire. But the entrance door was tightly locked. I wanted to kick the door until it burst open. I looked at the burned warehouse across the streetcar tracks. The warehouse was hot in the summer and ice-cold in the winter. It was a playground for rats. Still there had been happiness there.

Now I was furious. "Oh! Father!" I cried. If he had seen what Junko had done to me, he would fly over to confront her. Sniffling, and swallowing some lumps, I cut across the streetcar tracks and trudged to the rear of the warehouse. I headed for the stream to pick up my laundry. The old outhouse still stood. How I wished it could speak. The shed saw and knew everything.

I went inside, tore a piece of paper from a magazine, and wadded it to make it soft. I wiped my eyes and blew my nose as hard as I could to shake off the accusation. We had lost our comfortable home, our friends, our clothes, and even our mother, but we would never, never give up the Kawashima family honor, nor could anyone take it away from us. Junko would not accuse me if Father and Mother were with us. "Ah! Father!" I cried. "Do you miss us as much as we miss you?"

Sniffling as I left the outhouse, I spotted a half-burned stick—Ko's fire stick. I picked it up, then I went around and gathered small wood blocks, for fuel, until the rucksack was almost filled. The wind from the field began to nip through my thin blouse and the sun was tilting westward as I folded the still-wet laundry and put it beneath the rucksack's cover flap. It was heavier now than when I came before noon. I leaned forward, holding the half-burned stick, and hastened to the streetcar stop. When I passed the neighborhood police post, I spontaneously turned around. Maybe the policeman who had helped me during and after the fire was there. He would know what to do about Junko's accusation.

An unfamiliar policeman was smoking and reading a newspaper. I stood silently until he raised his head. I bowed in greeting. "If you are peddling, no peddling is allowed here!" he said. "Go!" He puffed a cigarette.

A policeman should be alert and ready to help people, I thought angrily. But I said, "I am looking for a policeman." I gave his description.

"You mean, Sergeant Kudo. He is on the midnight shift this week." The policeman dropped his eyes to the newspaper. I left the post without telling him my name.

Ko was awake when I returned to the hospital. Though she was an invalid, just being with her gave me a sense of security. I unpacked the rucksack and hung the laundry to dry completely. I opened the window halfway then built a fire. When the bucket of water was hot, I gave Ko a sponge bath.

"Ah! It feels so good!" she said. I massaged her sides and shoulders, wishing the man's bed-clothes would dry so that Ko could be warm.

Some of the morning's watery soup was still in the mess kit. I added water and chopped daikon bits and cooked it slowly on the shichirin.

"You did not forget to visit the Masudas' niece?" Ko asked.

I said I had gone there, but I did not tell her what had happened. If I did, Ko would make me go right back to Junko's house and say, "Though we are at the bottom of the bottom, the Kawashima children would never steal, harm, or destroy things that belong to others! Our parents did not raise us that way!"

The daikons were almost soft. As soon as Hideyo got back, we would be ready to eat. I could not wait to see Hideyo's and Ko's surprised faces when I brought out a piece of cake for each one of us.

Mrs. Minato was glad when I came to her with hot water for tea. She said that Hideyo was in the newspaper. "Here." She pointed to the headline: COURAGEOUS YOUNG MAN CATCHES PROWLER. I asked if I could borrow the newspaper to show my family. She said, "Keep it."

"I have a little time until my brother's return," I said, offering to cook something easy and quick for her. She said fried noodles would make her very happy.

I followed Mrs. Minato's instructions when I fried the noodles. They looked so tasty that I wished I could feed them to Ko. I told Mrs. Minato I would return later to do her dishes and put her kettle on the shichirin for her after-supper tea.

"Just a moment." Mrs. Minato stopped me. "I cannot eat all these noodles. Give me a small plate and take the rest with you."

I said, "I'll accept a small portion for Ko. Hideyo and I have soup."

She said, "You are a growing girl, Ko needs lots of nourishment, and your brother must have more than just a bowl of soup."

I put some noodles on a flat wood scrap, and placed it on Ko's chest. As she ate with her left hand, she listened to me read the newspaper, telling how Hideyo caught the robber.

"You are doing well!" Hideyo marveled at Ko as he entered the room.

While we ate, we exchanged news of our activities. But I did not tell them about seeing Goro or about Junko's accusation. I told Hideyo, "Our sister insists that I go back to school tomorrow. She should not be left alone all day."

Ko butted in quickly before Hideyo was able to say a word. "I can manage. Little One has missed two days already. Remember the monthly tuition was paid in advance. She must not waste it." Her tone was weak, but very firm.

"I do not want to go to school. I will be miserable." I talked back, knowing this was my only chance. "I want to learn how to sew some garments to sell. Honorable Sister can teach me right here at the hospital."

"You are not ready for that. But you are ready to go to school tomorrow!" said Ko.

"I will not!" I snapped at her.

"You! Spoiled brat! Just think of all those wounded, the orphans, and the homeless. They would be glad to trade with you right now! We have food, a place to sleep, and we are together!

71

That you are able to go to school is a great blessing! Don't talk back!" Ko's voice became shaky with tears.

"Stop the argument!" Hideyo yelled. "I am tired and I need silence now." He put noodles into his mouth, then sipped the watery soup. Very slowly, Ko went back to feeding herself. I drank my soup. "Unexpected spread!" Hideyo said.

When everyone was through, I poured hot water into the soup bowls, wishing it were green tea. I crawled under the bed and brought out two pieces of cake. I put Ko's share on the wooden plate. "Get well fast, Honorable Sister," I said, but after the word battle with Ko, my cheerfulness was gone. I handed another piece to Hideyo.

"A piece of cake?" Hideyo was mystified. "Where did it come from?" He examined the cake from every angle, even sniffed it.

"It is real cake, Honorable Brother!" I chuckled. Ko was staring at hers as if she could not believe her eyes. It was a pleasure to watch their surprised faces. "Why don't you eat?" I asked.

"Where is yours?" asked Ko.

I crawled back under the bed. "See? I have my own." When I took a bite, the creamy frosting melted in my mouth. At the same time, my memory took me back to the bamboo grove. Every time Mother's friend Mrs. Joffe came over, she brought a homemade cake with creamy icing and lots of edible dried flowers on top.

Hideyo finally put a small portion into his mouth. "Ummmmmmm! Deeeeeelicious!" he exclaimed.

"How long has it been since we had a western-style cake?" asked Ko. Her eyes were still fixed on the cake. "It's so pretty. I hate to eat it."

"If you hate to eat the cake, I will eat it for you!" Hideyo joked. Ko put a small portion into her mouth.

"Why such a small bite?" I asked.

"To last longer," replied Ko. "Tell us, Little One. Where did you get these?"

I told them how the three pieces of cake had fallen into my hands. Hideyo said he wanted to go and meet Mrs. Minato and thank her for her generosity. "Wonderful idea," I said. I thought it would be a good chance to tell Hideyo what the Masudas' niece had said.

While preparing Ko for the night, I told her, "I will be gone quite a while to do our chores and Mrs. Minato's, too." Hideyo stacked the soup bowls on three flat wooden scraps and carried them down the hall. I followed him with our personal things that I had to wash daily. We left everything at the sink and went to see Mrs. Minato.

I served Mrs. Minato a cup of tea and gathered her dishes and cooking utensils. I asked if she had any laundry. She shook her head. Leaving Hideyo with her, I went to the sink, finished all the tasks, and washed myself.

When Hideyo came, I told him about seeing the man named Goro. Then I told him of Junko's accusations.

Hideyo's expression changed immediately. He tightened his lips and began breathing heavily.

"What can we do about it?" I asked. He bit his lower lip as if to control his rage. His eyes were focused somewhere in the space for deep thinking. After a while I broke the silence. "What can we do?"

"Right now?" he looked at me closely. "Let us sleep. We are all tired."

"Sleep!" I yelled. "I cannot sleep. We've been accused of killing and robbing. We've been accused of setting the fire. I want to clear our names! You must think hard now!"

"Keep your voice down," commanded Hideyo. "We must make our move extremely carefully. Theft, arson, and murder are serious offenses. How can you prove it was Goro you saw between the warehouse and the factory a couple evenings ago?"

"His back! It was slightly hunched. How could his neck get burned? He must have been injured by Ko's stick!"

"You must not accuse anyone unless you are sure of everything," said Hideyo. "That goes for Junko, too! Now let us get some sleep. We can think straight when we are calm. Let's keep these offensive charges to ourselves. If Ko finds out, she will crawl all the way to the Masudas', and with her temper, you never know what she will do to

Junko. Ko's recovery is most important to us now."

Hideyo stayed with me while I put away Mrs. Minato's eating utensils and made sure her charcoals were out. I told her I would do her corridor early in the morning. "School tomorrow." I frowned.

"An order from General Headquarters!" said Hideyo, standing still as a soldier, then saluting. Mrs. Minato laughed with delight.

Ko told me to prepare my school things in my rucksack. I also packed a small wrapping cloth with some of Ko's wares to sell after school. Hideyo promised to wake me when he got up so that I could finish all my chores before I left for school. He handed me streetcar fare, half price for students. When I crawled under Ko's bed, Hideyo was already snoring as if he had no worry in the world.

At School

The streetcar to Sagano was almost empty when I got on to go to school. I kept thinking about Junko Masuda's accusation. *Arson. Theft. Murder!* Suddenly I shuddered. What if the police never caught the real criminal? Would Ko and I be arrested on false charges? If only Father was here to help us.

The school building came into sight, and graceful Atago Mountain looked sleepy still. The conductor announced, "Sagano." I asked him the time. He glanced at his watch and said, "It's seven." I did not get off the streetcar. Instead I stayed on for four more stops and changed to another streetcar line that took me to the burned warehouse. I walked quickly down the tracks to the police post. If yesterday's lazy policeman had been telling the truth, Sergeant Kudo should still be there.

He was surprised to see me and asked what I was doing out at this time of day. I told him of the accusations. As he listened, the sergeant tilted his head, his face troubled, staring at me as if he could not believe what I was saying. He told me he had given Junko Masuda a full report of the incident when she arrived from Tokyo. He had informed her that police headquarters was investigating the case and that her aunt's and uncle's remains had been taken to the morgue for further study. Sergeant Kudo added, "Miss Masuda must know that you and your sister had nothing to do with the fire."

I asked Sergeant Kudo if he had heard about the cash box. He said no, and that the factory, the warehouse, and the Masudas' house had been guarded until the niece arrived.

The small round clock on the wall struck eight. Sergeant Kudo's shift was over. Yesterday's lazy policeman was parking his bicycle by the rear door. Sergeant Kudo asked me to wait for him out front so that he could walk with me to the streetcar stop.

While walking with the sergeant, I told him about following Goro. He said he would go to see Dr. Yamada before he went home. "Every bit of information helps," he said.

My heart beat louder and louder as I walked through the school gate. I wondered how the girls would react to my coming back to school. Though I was half deaf, I could hear their bumble-bee-like noise at the student entrance. There I had to change from the clogs Mrs. Yamada had given me to my indoor slippers. But I could not find my slippers on the shoe shelf. Usually I could spot them easily. Ko had made the slippers with dark-purple cloth and she had embroidered them with the Kawashima crest in yellow thread. I searched for my slippers in row after row with no luck. I did not want to be late for my English class, so I rushed to the classroom barefoot.

As I entered, the room was suddenly quiet, and ninety eyes stared at me. I could hear my own bare feet hitting the floor as I went to my seat. There was a torn notebook page on my desk scribbled with the words *"Banzai!* (Hurrah!) She has stopped coming to school!" I could sense those forty-five lips jeering at me. From my rucksack I pulled out my English reader and the spelling tablet that I had made by the stream. I purposely put them on top of the scribbled note. After the roll call, study began.

Our English teacher, Mr. Yoshida, was short and skinny. He always wore a baggy white shirt and a black tie. Today he slowly walked between the rows of desks, reading "Rip Van Winkle" aloud. I liked study sessions, the only time the girls did not pick on me. But today I wished class would end quickly.

As soon as the bell rang, I headed for the furnace room to see Mr. Naido, my only friend. When I first met him, he stuttered badly. So whenever I spoke to him I spoke very slowly, as if to say, I too have a speech problem. Now, almost two years later, he was able to talk to me, very slowly, with only a slight stutter.

Mr. Naido was not in the furnace room. In a corner there were bundled trash papers, neatly stacked. Next to this stack was a wooden bucket where he kept things the students threw away. I took out a scrap of paper and wrote him a note to let him know I had returned and would be back to see him after school.

My feet were cold. I headed again to the shoe shelves for my slippers. While searching carefully, I remembered how Ko had stayed up late braiding old rags she'd gathered from the university trash baskets. These she coiled and sewed onto the soles, using extrafine stitches to secure them so they would last longer and keep my feet warmer. Now she was lying helplessly in the hospital. I felt like crying aloud.

I knew very well that no other girl in the school would want to have a pair of slippers as humble as mine, but they were my treasured possessions. I wrote on the students' daily bulletin boards, asking if anyone had seen Kawashima Yoko's slippers and, if so, to please let her know. By the time the last school bell rang, my message had been erased.

I decided to leave my rucksack in the furnace room from then on, as I felt it would be safe there. Mr. Naido's eyes lit up when he saw me. He said he'd been worried about me ever since he learned about the clog-factory fire. "I . . . am glad you are back," he said very slowly but excitedly. "I . . . saved you papers! H-here are w-w-atercolors! I . . . even saved you reference books! T-tell me, w-w-where do you live now?"

I spoke extra slowly. "I have no time to talk. My group has been assigned to clean the south-wing bathroom. I will be back as soon as the cleaning is over."

There were twelve toilets. There was also a large, oblong tile basin with four water faucets. The weekly duty teacher would go around to inspect the cleaning. If the job was not done well, we would have to do it over again. None of us would be allowed to go home until we passed the cleaning inspection.

I was the first one there. No one came as I

cleaned the first six toilets. I kept on with the seventh and the eighth. Still no one came.

The inspecting teacher, Mr. Iwai, arrived. He was tall, with pomade-shined black hair. His eyes were bad and he wore thick lenses. "Are you alone? Where are the rest of the girls?" he asked.

"I do not know, sir."

"Who is in your group?"

I named five girls. We had cleaned the teachers' room last week. Without a word, he took off in quick steps. I kept on working. The faster I got it done, the quicker I could get back to Ko.

About the time Mr. Iwai brought the five girls to help with the cleaning, I was putting the bucket and rags away. Mr. Iwai made the girls stand in a row. I stood at the end. He inspected the twelve toilets and the basin.

"I have checked your group's schedule. You were here yesterday, and the day before. Why not today?" No one answered.

But I immediately knew why. They did not want to be with me. Besides, for two days I had been absent and they had done my share.

"I am asking! Why not today?" questioned Mr. Iwai. One girl said, in a muffled voice, she had extra homework. Mr. Iwai snapped back, "Homework must be done *after* the cleaning." He yelled the word *after*.

"What is your next excuse?" No one answered. Mr. Iwai paced back and forth in front of us. He stopped in front of me and said, "You may go home."

On the way to the furnace room to get my rucksack, I met Miss Asada, my homeroom teacher. She said I had not presented a guardian's written statement explaining my absence. If I had been ill, I needed a doctor's note. I told her I would bring it tomorrow.

My conversation with Mr. Naido took a long time. I told him about everything, including the false accusation. "I have been studying how to clear it! But I do not know where to begin. I need Father, but I do not know how or where to look for him." He listened with compassion, then handed me an old wrapping cloth with the goods he had saved for me.

I carried my rucksack on my back and held the wrapping cloth tightly under my right arm as I left the furnace room. But I turned around and asked Mr. Naido to keep his eyes open for my school slippers.

"I bet the girls took them!" he yelled in anger. Every time he got mad at the girls, he spoke perfectly. I wondered, if he were angry at everybody and every day, would he perhaps get over his stuttering? At such a thought I smiled. "You are smiling," he said. "There is nothing funny about them hiding your slippers!"

It was too late to start selling Ko's wares now. I watched the sunset from the streetcar window and wondered how Ko and Mrs. Minato had gotten through the day without my help.

Just in case Ko was asleep, I quietly entered her room, but she said, "Welcome home!" There was forced energy in her tone. "How did you do? Were you able to catch up?"

"Of course!" I put on a good front. "But I forgot to bring the absence excuse. How did you manage without your faithful nurse?"

"Just fine! But I cannot hold on anymore!" I dropped my belongings and helped Ko with the bedpan. Then I gave her a sponge bath. Now the bedclothes were completely dry. I put them on Ko with great difficulty. With the plaster casts on her arm and legs, she seemed to weigh a ton.

"Thanks! I feel much better!" Ko closed her puffy, black eyes. I boiled water for Ko to drink. All she had eaten for lunch were leftover noodles that I'd put on the wooden plate and left on her chest before I went to school.

While Ko was drinking hot water, I went to Mrs. Minato's and made her a cup of tea.

"I was very dry. I was afraid to get out of bed. I felt dizzy all day," she said. She asked about my school.

I told her that if I could have my way, I would stay away. "I hate it!" She laughed and said she had felt the same when she was young because she could not sit still.

I asked if her husband or friends had come to see her during the day. She said she had not heard from her husband since he'd gone to war. "The war has been over for two years. I worry about him." She sighed deeply. I was sorry I had mentioned her husband. She said that from now on her meals would be brought to her by her mother's neighbor. "Oh, yes!" she exclaimed, and asked me how much she owed me for cleaning her room and corridor. I told her she did not owe me anything, but I would be very happy if she would give me some tea leaves and some salt.

I did not have to think what to cook for our supper. I boiled daikon greens and chopped them. I added a bit of salt to the green water, wishing I had tofu or seaweed to make it tastier. Ko would get well in no time with more nutritious food.

Hideyo came home with a large codfish head. He said he had passed a fish market and seen a man throwing some heads away, so he picked one up thinking it would give us some protein. Hideyo split the cod head in half. I put the first half into the green water and boiled it. Ko told me to heavily salt the other half and broil part of it on the shichirin for tomorrow's meal.

We wholeheartedly enjoyed the fish head soup and some weak tea. Ko said, "Save the used tea leaves and dry them. We can use them in the future."

Hideyo told us he wanted to go and get his own bedding from Dr. Yamada's shed. "I was very cold during the night. The fall is getting deeper."

"I will go with you," I said. I needed to speak

with Hideyo about my talk with Sergeant Kudo.

"You should stay and give our sister her bath and prepare her for the night," Hideyo said.

"I already did," I answered. Then I lied, "I need my school slippers from the shed."

"I will bring them to you."

"You do not know where they are."

"I will find them. Tell me where you put them," said Hideyo.

I said, "Everything is all mixed up. I must look for them myself."

Ko motioned me to come near her. She said she wanted me to bring a book called *Bochan,* which she had borrowed from her university library. She wanted her shoes, too.

"Your shoes?" questioned Hideyo.

"It's too cold for Little One to wear clogs. Her toes freeze from the least chill," said Ko. "She can put on a few pairs of socks and wear my shoes."

I crawled under Ko's bed and picked up the half-burned stick and Mr. Naido's old wrapping cloth.

"Why are you taking a stick?" asked Hideyo.

"So I can shoo a dog that chases me."

As soon as we were out on the street, Hideyo said, "I called Dr. Yamada from a public telephone during my lunch break to thank him for all he has done. The doctor told me to come see him this evening because Sergeant Kudo has begun to investigate a man named Goro. So I made an excuse to go after my futon and beddings,"

Hideyo explained. "I will need them sooner or later anyway, and you need your comforter."

"I brought this stick," I said, waving it in the chilly night air, "because Ko poked someone with it. Maybe the doctor can examine Goro's wound. If the wound matches the stick, then he was at the outhouse."

The doctor was still working. I held the Yamadas' flashlight while Hideyo bundled his futon in the shed. I packed the things Ko had asked me to get and as many daikon greens as I could fit into a wrapping cloth.

We were about to go to the doctor's residence when I saw the shadow of a short, stout, and slightly hunchbacked man on the frosted glass. Goro! I got excited. I shook Hideyo's left arm. "That is the man," I said in Korean, because I did not want the shadow to know what I was saying. When Hideyo looked, the shadow had vanished. Hideyo quickly took off, and I followed. We stood at the corner of the building and peeked. The man's face showed clearly under the bright entrance light. It was not Goro. He did not have a bandage around his neck. Instead, the man had a huge patch on the left side of his face. He did not notice us, and slowly walked off toward the general store, dragging the heels of very shiny, knee-high rubber boots.

"That's strange," Hideyo murmured. "I am going to follow him. Go and ask the doctor to come out."

Hideyo came back holding a dripping-wet handkerchief. It smelled terrible. "What in the world is that?" asked the doctor. "Don't tell me you washed your hanky in the gutter!"

"Will you please open the clinic entrance?" said Hideyo in great agitation. "I want to check on something."

As soon as the door was opened and the light was turned on, Hideyo looked for something on the concrete floor. He found wet shoe prints where the patients took off their shoes to enter the examination room.

"What are you looking for?" questioned Dr. Yamada. Mrs. Yamada and I were mystified, too.

"I wanted to know if your patient's boots were wet. If they were wet, perhaps the water came from the gutter." Hideyo asked for tissue paper and let it soak up the water from the concrete. He asked for small boxes, and carefully placed the wet tissue paper in one box, and his smelly handkerchief in the other. He said he was going to take them to Sergeant Kudo later and ask to have a laboratory test done.

Hideyo made an apology for disturbing the doctor, but said he wanted to know all about the man who had left the office earlier with a patch on his left cheek.

"He is Morita. He is visiting a friend here, or so I heard." The doctor looked at us with curious eyes. He said, "Sergeant Kudo came this morning and asked me many questions about Goro's burn.

What has Goro or Morita got to do with you?"

"My little sisters are charged with arson, theft, and murder," said Hideyo, explaining how distressed we were. "We want to clear our names as fast as we can. We can't let Ko find out!" Hideyo went on, "Did Morita tell you how he hurt his face?"

The doctor and Mrs. Yamada were shocked by Junko's false accusation and their mouths hung open for a while, but the doctor finally said, "Morita mentioned he was lighting some fireworks to show his friend's children, and sparks exploded near his face."

"What does Goro's neck wound look like? Was it poked by something long and sharp?" I asked. The doctor shook his head. "The wound looked as though some hot grease was splashed on his neck. It was not a bad burn."

Dr. Yamada asked Hideyo why he wanted the samples of tissue paper and wet handkerchief to be examined.

"When Morita left the clinic, I noticed his shiny rubber boots. I had never seen rubber boots so shiny, but quickly realized they shone because they were wet. The man could not have gone fishing at this time of night. If he had been fishing, his boots would have been dry, because it has been dark for hours and all fishermen quit fishing in time to get home by dark. So I followed the guy." Hideyo continued, "Morita came to the tenement area where the open gutter runs. He walked slowly along the gutter for a while. He stopped. Then he put his one leg in the gutter as if to wash the boot in the smelly water. But he did not do the same with the other. He backtracked to the narrow, winding road. I followed him to the house where he entered. I then went to the gutter to wet my handkerchief."

"What does that prove?" asked Dr. Yamada.

"I do not know now. I only know that some people do strange things," said Hideyo. He looked very serious.

Hideyo's words *tenement* and *gutter* made my mind race; that was where I had lost sight of Goro. The doctor had said "fireworks," but I knew that fireworks were only for summer, by permit, in an open field. Was it Morita who was in the outhouse and poked by Ko's fire stick? I wondered. I asked the doctor when Morita first came for treatment. He asked Mrs. Yamada to get the medical log.

"He came Monday night. At eight forty-five."

"Let me show you the burned stick," I said. Hurriedly I went to the shed to get it. "My sister poked someone with this stick, and the end of it was burning. I heard a man scream."

"Hmm!" the doctor said, and crossed his arms, thinking. He then took hold of the stick. After examining it with his thumbnail, he ordered his wife to bring him glass slides. "This looks like human skin," the doctor said, carefully putting it between the slides. "Let me send all the samples to the laboratory, stick and all!" He telephoned Sergeant Kudo to come and pick up some very important objects.

LOOSE MORALS?

Because Hideyo and I did not get back from Dr. Yamada's until way after midnight, I was still sleepy when Hideyo woke me at five-thirty. I whipped myself to finish the chores for Ko and Mrs. Minato. Ko insisted that I put on two pairs of socks and her shoes before I left for school. For still-sleepy me, Ko's large black, weather-beaten leather shoes were hard and heavy. Still, at school I stuffed Ko's shoes into my rucksack and left them with Mr. Naido, for fear someone would take them.

Miss Asada looked at my absence excuse, written by Hideyo. He had used Father's seal to make it official. She read it, added her own seal, and told me to take the note to the principal. Just as I was entering the principal's office, I met Mr. Naido bringing in a large tea tray. I opened the door for him. In his slow-speaking manner, Mr. Naido greeted the principal, who ignored him. The principal was reading the morning paper. Mr. Naido poured the tea and started to straighten up the room.

I bowed deeply to the principal, but said nothing. I did not want Mr. Naido to find out that I could speak normally. I put the note in front of the principal so that he could read and seal the document. Then I would take it to the school clerk to be filed.

The bald-headed principal gave me a stern look through his rimless half lenses. "Sit down!" he ordered sharply. He did not even look at the absence excuse. "Where did you sleep last night?"

Mr. Naido stopped cleaning ashtrays and stood still. His worried eyes met mine. I did not answer.

"Answer my question!" the principal shouted. "Or are you too ashamed to talk?"

Ashamed? I was still tired, so I wondered if I heard him well. I tilted my good ear toward him to hear better.

"Don't act like an innocent maiden. You are shaming my school!"

I spoke extremely slowly and asked, "Shame? What did I do wrong, sir?"

"You know that yourself. I want to know where you went and where you slept last night! Tell me the truth."

"Tell you the truth, sir?"

"Don't pretend! I will tell you, then." He said he had received a telephone call from a woman a while ago. She said she had seen me walking with a man late last night.

I answered slowly. "I went to see Dr. Yamada with my brother."

He gave me a sneering smile. "Don't lie!" he said. "When they are caught, everyone makes excuses saying he was a brother, an uncle, or even a distant cousin!" He thumbed through several documents. "When your mother filled out the forms, she put down that you were separated from your father and brother." The principal went on, "The voice on the telephone told me that the Kawashima girls are very loose and that their mother has never been home. I must have a talk with your mother. Tell her to come see me tomorrow."

Mr. Naido dropped an ashtray and stared at me. He knew Mother was dead. The principal ordered him to leave. Mr. Naido apologized for making noise. He poured another cup of tea and said slowly that he had a little more to straighten up. "Then do it quickly and get out," shouted the principal. He sipped his tea loudly, but his angry eyes were fixed on me through his half lenses.

The moment the principal mentioned Mother, the unbearable memory of how she had left me forever at the train station became vivid in my mind. I held back my tears as best I could. "Mother cannot come," I said, and I bit my lips. If the principal ever found out that Mother was dead and that Ko and I had been without a male guardian until Hideyo's return, he might suspend me from the school for good. I could not let my sister and brother down.

"Why can't your mother come?" the principal demanded.

"She is not with us right now."

"Where did she go?"

I could not answer.

"Where did she go?" the principal threw the question sharply again. His sharpness reminded me of the army policeman who had beaten me up in Nanam, and what I was about to say made me terribly sad.

"Since my brother is home now, Mother went to her *home*." By *home*, I meant Paradise. "Please, telephone Dr. Yamada's residence. He or Mrs. Yamada will verify that we were there."

The principal had his secretary call Dr. Yamada. While listening to the doctor over the phone, he searched on the desk for Hideyo's handwritten note.

Mr. Naido, wearing a smile, bowed to the principal and said, "Everything is straightened out, sir!" He silently closed the office door behind him.

"You may go," said the principal to me in normal tones. He shoved the absence excuse at me. But I sat there. "I said *go!*" he hollered.

I hated the way he turned up his nose at me. I thought he owed me an apology for thinking me a girl of loose morals. Then, too, I was boiling mad at the woman who had telephoned the school. Maybe it was Junko, I thought. When I asked, the principal said, "The woman did not identify herself. Now go! I have much to do!"

I did not like his yelling. I did not move. "Are

you deaf?" he screamed. This made me furious. It was not my fault that I had lost half my hearing! It happened when a bomb dropped while we were fleeing. I almost shouted at him, *"Yes!"* Besides, a year and a half ago this man had opened a personal letter to me from Corporal Matsumura without my permission. The thought that he had been so rude and had never even apologized made my blood boil. I sat still and stared. The principal slapped a ruler on his desk and again yelled, "Go!"

"You owe me an apology, sir," I said straight-forwardly.

"No, I do not! You should be glad I am concerned about my students."

"I do not appreciate it."

"You smart aleck. Where is your respect for your principal?" Our angry eyes met.

"Respect is to be gained, not demanded!" My voice was firm and clear. I picked up Hideyo's note, quickly stood, and left the office without bowing.

I could not concentrate on my studies that day. I was hurt by the principal's charge, and the more I thought of the woman caller, the more my anger raged. I wanted to scream and scream until the roof blew off the school. Whoever she was, I would find her if it took me the rest of my life!

After school I was sorting trash in the furnace room. Mr. Naido came pushing his wooden cart. I thanked him for trying to stay with me in the principal's office. He smiled and said, "Y-y-y-you done good, there!"

He gave me five yen and said it was for the cans I had brought for him to sell before the fire. I said I could not have made that much from twenty-two cans. He said he had added his cans to mine. He also said he had seen a sign at the butcher's shop that giblets were on sale, so I must get some. "A sick young woman needs nourishing food."

Instead of selling handicrafts, I went straight back to the hospital with the giblets. I was shocked to see Ko, flat on her back, holding a summer kimono between her teeth, carefully taking the seams apart with a razor blade.

"What are you doing?" I exclaimed. "You should be resting!"

"It's making me crazy to lie here. I had to do something," said Ko.

"Your face is swollen like a balloon. Who handed you the kimono from my futon?"

"I asked the nurse who came to take my temperature," said Ko. She closed her eyes and took a deep but depressed sigh. Then I cleared away what she had scattered on her chest.

While giving her a sponge bath I remembered all the unpleasantness that had dropped on me like a bomb in school, including the sharp words of the principal. "I don't want to go to school anymore!" I said. Ko asked why. "I do not like the atmosphere." I frowned.

"Nothing is wrong with the school. The students make the atmosphere. You are one of the students who makes it! Instead of complaining, why don't you become a leader and change it? Brother has been working hard to pay for your schooling!"

"You want to tell me I cannot waste the tuition money, right? Every second word with you is *money,* and I am sick and tired of hearing it!" I dashed out to the corridor, slamming the sliding door behind me as hard as I could. "She doesn't know what's going on at the school!" I grumbled.

I went outside to calm myself. Already the maples were turning a bright red and some of the leaves were dancing in the wind and sailing to the ground. I picked several small leaves and ate one. It tasted tender. Though I was still angry, I thought, "If I had a cup of oil and some flour, I could make Ko maple-leaf tempuras."

Mrs. Minato was glad to see me. She said she had seen me picking leaves. I asked if someone had brought her supper. If they had not, I would offer to make tempuras. At the same time I was going to ask her to let me use the oil. She said she had already had her supper, but whenever I finished the evening chores, she would love to have some hot, strong green tea. I asked about the best way to cook giblets, to give the most nourishment to my sick sister. "Stir-fry. But be sure to slice the giblets thin and fry them before you add vegetables," she said. "Sesame oil would give the best flavor."

"I have no sesame oil. Is there any other way?" I asked. She told me there was oil, seasoning, and dried groceries in the portable cupboard which sat on the floor. "It will be easier for you to clean my room if you take it all."

Ko was not talking. She did not even look at the portable cupboard I had just inherited.

I cooked the giblets and sampled them. They tasted mighty good. I dished a small portion onto the wooden scrap plate and put it on Ko's chest. "Honorable Sister, try this. It is delicious."

Her swollen eyes stared at me. A string of tears ran down her cheek. I realized what I had done. "I was rude. I am sorry," I apologized.

She then ordered me to demonstrate how to open and close the door elegantly.

"I am correcting your manner. If Brother or I do not guide you, then who will?"

"*Wakatta!* I understand!" I answered. Ko then picked up the giblet stir-fry with her good fingers and tasted. "Excellent, Little One! Excellent!" Her voice quivered with tears.

While waiting for Hideyo's return I read to Ko from *Bochan*. Hearing some funny sentences, she laughed. Though her face was swollen and ugly, how beautiful she looked when she laughed. I decided to borrow more funny books from the city library. Maybe she would recover faster.

Hideyo was happy to hear Ko welcome him home. "I am starved!" he said, and went to the wooden sink to wash. I put the book away and prepared for us to eat.

"Are you catching up with your schoolwork?" Hideyo asked during dinner. I nodded. Hideyo said he had checked with the nurses and had learned that Ko was progressing slowly but well.

"It is good news to hear," Ko said. "But the longer I stay, the more the bill piles up."

Nothing but bad things had happened since we left our home in Korea. Still, being with Ko and Hideyo in the evening made me feel extremely secure, and I realized our togetherness each day was precious in hours, minutes, and moments.

The ground was already frosted in mid-November. Because my school slippers were gone, I walked barefoot inside the school. I was not about to ruin my socks because I needed them to fit into Ko's shoes. As the day went by, my toes lost their feeling and my whole abdomen ached. During recess I went to the furnace room to warm my feet. Often Mr. Naido was not there, but I kept myself busy sorting discarded magazines, newspapers, notebooks, and school supplies from his wooden cart. I took what I could use, as Mr. Naido wished.

One day Mr. Naido asked if I would be interested in earning about twenty yen. Why, I had never earned that much at once! I could not believe my ears. Mr. Naido said, "It is an unpleasant job."

"No matter what type of job it is, as long as it's honest money, I am proud to work," I said.

He said, "The farmers have come to clean out the toilets."

As we worked outside the toilet building, several girls stood in a circle watching us scoop the human waste from the septic tank. Some put their handkerchiefs over their mouths and noses. Some giggled and made faces.

The farmers, Mr. Naido, and I kept on. When one tub was filled, a farmer carted it away while the rest of us began filling another empty tub. Suddenly, just as Mr. Naido poured his dipperful of waste into the empty tub, he yelled, "No!"

I looked up to see one of my slippers about to slide into the tub! "My slipper!" I screamed for gladness. But I realized it was already ruined. I wanted to dump whoever did this into the farmer's tub. In anger I worked faster. When we finished the job, Mr. Naido gave me my earnings and lots of small, thin pieces of soap that he had saved from the school basins. "It's getting d-d-dark," he said. "H-h-h-h-hurry home now."

Ko had been hospitalized for fifty-eight days. When the chief surgeon last examined her he'd said, "She is doing all right." I asked when Ko's swollen face, hand, and toes would go back to normal.

"Maybe in a couple of weeks. . . . I hope so." Then he added, "Your sister is fortunate that she did not break her neck. Keep her warm and give her plenty of fluids." Already late, I rushed home to take care of Ko.

Mrs. Minato was visiting her, and when I went to fetch some water for their tea, I saw a man standing in the corridor. He had a piece of paper and was checking Ko's name tag on the door. It was the police inspector. He recognized me.

Why was he looking for Ko? Something awful must have happened to Hideyo! My heart raced, and my mouth dried. I went to him fast and whispered that Ko was very ill, that I did not want him to give her bad news. However, if he had to, would he please be as gentle as possible? He said he had come to ask her some questions.

"Don't you know that Junko Masuda has officially pressed charges against you and your sister?" said the inspector.

I told him Ko did not know that Junko Masuda had made groundless accusations against us.

"What's going on?" Ko called.

I looked at the inspector and silently begged him not to tell Ko. Then I said, "The police inspector has come to see you."

Mrs. Minato bowed slightly to the inspector and asked me to walk her to her room. I hurried back as the inspector was showing Ko his police badge and identification card.

"Has something happened to Brother?" she asked fearfully.

"Nothing has happened to your brother. But I came to ask you few questions," he said. Ko let out a happy sigh. The inspector asked Ko if she could identify the man she hit with the fire stick. She said it was dark and it happened so quickly and unexpectedly, and she was so frightened, that she did not see his face. However, she said, she could identify the man by his "screaming voice."

"Do you think you might have poked him in the face?" questioned the inspector.

"Not in the face. Unless he was shorter than I."

"How tall are you?"

"One hundred and eighty centimeters. Why?"

The inspector folded his arms, tilted his head and nodded to himself. He said he wanted to speak with Hideyo that evening at the police laboratory.

Ko asked, "Why can't you talk to me now? What is the connection between Hideyo and the police laboratory?"

Nervous that the inspector might tell Ko about the charges, I gave him a steady stare.

The inspector said that he wanted to tell Hideyo that Mr. and Mrs. Masuda were already dead before the fire.

Ko's and my shocked eyes met. I opened my mouth to say something, but I could not utter a word. Ko said, "What has been bothering me is, Why were they in the factory at that late hour?"

"We do not know. One thing we do know is,

whoever killed them must have known their schedule well." Then the inspector added, "Dr. Yamada, Sergeant Kudo, and the medical examiner will be at the police laboratory at eight-thirty tonight. We would like your brother to be there."

The nurse came in to check on Ko. The inspector wished her a speedy recovery and made a quick exit, leaving me up in the air. He had not come just to question Ko. He was hiding some important information. Just a few moments ago, thinking how tall Ko was, he had folded his arms, tilted his head, and nodded to himself, meaning he was convinced about something.

I caught up with the inspector at the hospital entrance and asked him if I could come to the laboratory with Hideyo. "I want to learn more about Mr. and Mrs. Masuda's death," I said.

"It is not a pleasant place to visit," he replied in an official tone. "But come if you must."

I knew that if I didn't finish my evening chores and prepare Ko for the night before Hideyo came home, he would never agree to let me go with him.

Ko told me I must cook the rest of a salted codfish head that we had been saving. Then she murmured to herself, "How wonderful it would be to have hot fluffy rice to go with the broiled fish head." I said, "I will go buy a cup of rice using some of the wrapping-cloth money."

"No! Don't touch that money. It is strictly for emergencies," said Ko.

"This *is* an emergency. You'll get well quicker if you eat better."

"I am better. Never touch the wrapping-cloth money!"

Suddenly I remembered that I had my earnings from scooping out the toilets at school. I took the twenty yen out of my rucksack. "I will be back soon," I said, practically flying to a rice shop I'd seen nearby.

On the wooden plate I dished up some fluffy rice and some of the broiled salted codfish head. I brought it to Ko's chest. She was staring at the plate. "Where did you get the money to buy rice?" asked Ko. I told her how I had earned it. "You must learn to save and manage the money. We can live without rice!" said my big sister.

AT THE POLICE LABORATORY

After supper, Hideyo announced that he would soon leave for the police laboratory.

"I am going with you, Honorable Brother!" I said excitedly. Ko shook her head and told me

I should wash the still-unattended summer kimonos. I said, "I will do all the washing tomorrow very early." Ko shook her head again as if to say, Do what I tell you.

"But I want to know how Mr. and Mrs. Masuda died," I argued. "The inspector said I may come."

"Let the police handle these matters. Mind your own business," said Ko.

"I am curious," I answered. Besides, I thought, it is my business to clear our names.

"That's the trouble with you," Ko said in disgust. "Not only are you strong-willed—you are strong-headed and stubborn!"

"Curious, yes! Persistent, yes! Stubborn, yes! But I am not strong-willed or strong-headed!" My voice was getting louder and louder.

"Behave yourselves!" Hideyo ordered. "I did not come home to hear you argue. This room is supposed to be our peaceful home."

I begged Hideyo to take me with him.

"There is nothing you can do there. You take care of Ko," he said.

"I already did. I want to learn things," I said, giving Hideyo a look that meant I really wanted to go.

"You will probably faint when you see the dead bodies," Hideyo said.

"I know you will faint," Ko said. "Stay here."

"I will not faint," I argued.

So Hideyo gave a warning, "If you do faint, you will spend the night among the bodies, because I am too exhausted to carry you home."

The inspector met us at the information office and led us to the laboratory. There was incense burning at the entrance to the morgue. Hideyo and I followed Japanese tradition and offered fresh incense and prayed that the deceased souls would rest in peace.

The laboratory looked like an operating room in a hospital. Huge, bright lights were suspended from the ceiling. Lots of medical instruments were neatly arranged in white metal-and-glass cabinets. A high, narrow wooden table alongside the window was filled with large jars of alcohol and preserved human organs. The old wooden floor was stained and scratched. I shivered at the peculiar smell.

Dr. Yamada, Sergeant Kudo, and a medical examiner were waiting for us. As the inspector opened a large wooden door with the largest steel handle I had ever seen, cold air swept out. The inspector urged us all to go in and he closed the door quickly behind us. The dark room had the strong smell of disinfectant. Gradually my eyes became used to the surroundings. There were huge blocks of ice stacked around the walls.

"We call this the ice room," said the inspector.

There were bodies on the tables, covered with a canvaslike gray material. A name tag hung from each cover. From the shapes of the covers it looked as though some of the bodies were sound asleep, some stretching their arms, some pulling their knees up high. Some looked as though they would jump up at any moment. In spite of the cold, my mouth was dry and I wanted a drink of water.

The medical examiner motioned for us to come over. "Stay here," whispered Hideyo. I held his hand tightly and pulled him to stay with me by the door. But Hideyo shook off my hand and went toward the tables. I held on to the door handle so that if the dead arose I could dash out of the room.

The examiner uncovered two tables that were pulled together. In a small space between Hideyo and Dr. Yamada I saw a burned arm and hand. The examiner explained: "Mr. Masuda received a blow behind his right ear from a heavy hammerlike tool. He died instantly. Here is the spot." He went on, saying, "Mrs. Masuda was also hit by the same weapon, on the forehead. She must have scratched someone violently. Her nails were bent and held skin particles. We know she was still alive when the fire started because her lungs were filled with smoke."

Scared as I was, I could not hold back my tears. I remembered how Mrs. Masuda's warm arms wrapped around me when Mother's body slid into the mouth of the furnace that Ko courageously lit for the cremation. Now she was cold and stiff. Her brutally beaten and burned body was on the table and the police could not say who had done it or why.

I was glad when we returned to the bright laboratory. Though it was not heated, how warm it felt!

"How about the results of the tests on the samples we sent in?" asked Dr. Yamada.

The examiner flipped through his sheaf of papers. He said, "The substance on the burned stick was indeed human skin. It matched Morita's facial-skin sample, which Dr. Yamada sent in later on. The sewer water on the handkerchief and the tissue paper also matched. So, it was Morita who was in the outhouse.

"Have you checked the skin particles in Mrs. Masuda's nails?" asked the inspector. "Did they match with Morita's?"

The examiner answered, "No, they did not match at all." The examiner said his sixth sense told him there was another person involved.

"We have a big case here," said the police inspector. "We now have a suspect, but how are we going to handle the charges against the Kawashima girls?"

Hideyo was distressed and asked, "Do you have to arrest my sisters?"

"Arrest me and Ko . . . am I to go to a jail?" I

yelled. I had only seen a jail in pictures. A dark, small cubicle, barred and heavily locked. Suddenly I was overcome by fright and fainted.

I came to my senses on the tall, narrow table in the laboratory. Dr. Yamada was massaging my chest. How many dead people had been put on that same table? I sat up quickly and was about to jump down, but was halted by the doctor. The medical examiner handed me a glass of water.

"Are you going to put me in jail?" I asked fearfully.

"You will continue your schooling as if nothing has happened," said the police inspector. "We will try to find those who did it."

"Nasty charges are hanging over me and my big sister. I hate this," I said. "I want to help investigate. I want to clear the Kawashima name as fast as I can."

The police inspector told Sergeant Kudo, "Watch every move Morita makes. He is our number-one suspect."

"But Morita told Dr. Yamada he was hurt by fireworks," I said.

"So Morita said when he came to my office," said Dr. Yamada. "He could be lying."

"How about Goro?" I said. "He went to see the doctor saying he burned his neck the night of the fire. My hunch is that he was the one who was walking between the factory and the warehouse. The way he vanished so quickly when I called my brother's name meant he was where he should not have been. Otherwise, he would have said something like, 'I am not your brother, but good evening,' no?" They all nodded, but it was Morita's skin that was on the stick.

"I want to reexamine Goro's neck," said Dr. Yamada. He asked the medical examiner to go with him to the ice room to get more skin from Mrs. Masuda's fingernails for testing.

The police inspector ordered Sergeant Kudo to check the police log to see if a fireworks permit had been issued in the ten days before the fire. When Hideyo and I were about to leave the laboratory, the inspector said, "The truth always comes up in the end. Carry on!"

Ko awaited our return. She wanted to know all about it. "I could not sleep," she said. Except for telling her about the charges against us, Hideyo told her almost everything.

"So, our Little One did not faint," Ko said.

"Ah, about the Little One," said Hideyo as he crawled into his futon. "She was fantastic!" I was glad the room was dim, so that Ko could not see Hideyo's cunning smile.

When I scooted under Ko's cot to sleep, I gently touched the wrapping-cloth bundle. I thanked Mother for looking after us and begged, if her spirit could fly, that she would go now and search for Father and tell him to come back quickly to his children.

WATCH MISSING

Knowing the police were working to find the killers, I was able to concentrate on the *Tale of Genji*, the classic, at school. I wished that there was no recess and that Mrs. Ando would keep on teaching so that the girls would not pick on me. But as soon as she left the classroom, Kyoko exclaimed, "Everyone! Listen! We have a thief in the class." A loud stir arose in the room.

"Don't you all know Kawashima Yoko is a thief?" Kyoko added. "It was in the morning paper. She was charged on three counts—murder, arson, stealing. My mother said I must protect my belongings from now on." All the girls stared at me.

Astonished to learn that such an article was in the paper, I shouted, "The police know I am innocent. They are looking for the criminal!"

"She is lying. The newspaper always prints the truth—especially from the police headquarters," yelled Kyoko. Everyone began to shove their coin purses into their schoolbags.

Just last night the police inspector had said I would continue my schooling as if nothing had happened. I thought they were protecting me. Instead, they released my name to the papers. Humiliated, hurt, and angry, I ran to the furnace room. I asked Mr. Naido if he had read about me in the morning paper. I explained to him what had gone on at the police laboratory the night before. He left right away to get the paper from the teachers' room. The bell for the next class rang before Mr. Naido returned, so I headed to the gymnasium, wondering why the police had to tell everything to a newspaper reporter.

The other students were gathered in the gymnasium, wearing dark blue bloomers. I owned no bloomers, so I rolled up my trousers knee high and stood in line. The gym teacher, Miss Yajima, fresh from the university, was practicing ballet steps in toe shoes. She wore a long, dark-blue, pleated skirt that, when she raised her leg high, opened as a fan. Around her neck hung a metal whistle. When she saw us standing, she called the roll. Kyoko was not there.

While we were doing routine exercises, Kyoko showed up, still wearing her dress. "What is your excuse?" asked Miss Yajima. Kyoko said she was extremely sorry, but she had lost her watch and was searching for it. I noticed that one of the large red ribbons that tied her looped braided hair at the neck was missing. Around her left wrist hung a beautiful purse. Bringing unnecessary personal belongings to school was against the rules in the student handbook, but Kyoko didn't care. She frowned and sat on a bench for the rest of the class.

After gym I took fast steps to the chemistry room. I wanted to take a seat in the very front row so that I could hear Mrs. Tsuda's soft voice. She was already there. I bowed to her, then sat and waited for my classmates.

The girls did not come for a long time. When they finally showed up, everyone was circling Kyoko, talking. They took seats way in the back of the room, still talking. Mrs. Tsuda ordered them to be silent and said, "Come to the front." But no one made a move. There was a big space between me and the other girls.

The principal came in. He whispered something to Mrs. Tsuda. Then I was called to step outside. The principal grabbed hold of my left arm and marched me to his office.

"Sit down!" he commanded angrily, looking at me over his half glasses. "Miss Sawayama reported her watch missing. She said she was pretty sure you stole it. Because you took off in a hurry after gym, she thought you might have hidden it somewhere."

I told him why I had rushed to the chemistry class. "I was there before anyone," I said.

The principal said, "Mrs. Tsuda verified that." But he asked, "Where did you go between the gymnasium and the chemistry room?"

"Nowhere," I said.

He stared at me doubtfully. How I hated his look! I felt like grabbing his glasses, throwing them on the floor, and stamping them to pieces. "Where is your schoolbag?" asked the principal.

"In the furnace room, sir."

"Why did you leave your belongings there?" he asked.

"They are safe there." I told him that someone had dumped my indoor slippers in the toilet.

The principal took me to the furnace room. Mr. Naido was sorting trash and some bits were ready for burning. He bowed to the principal and asked him politely what he could do to help. The principal asked where my belongings were. Mr. Naido got my rucksack from a locked utility closet and was about to hand it to me.

"Naido! Dump everything," the principal ordered.

Mr. Naido gave me a compassionate look and untied the rucksack. I had not had so many papers and books when I came to school that morning. He must have gathered them for me, I thought, as he took out each item. Lastly he took out Ko's shoes. Now the rucksack was completely empty. The principal shook the shoes and examined the rucksack's little pockets. He found a few coins.

"Where did you get this?" asked the principal.

"It is my streetcar fare."

"What are you looking for, sir?" asked Mr. Naido.

"An Omega watch. Belonging to Sawayama Kyoko."

The principal checked through every loose paper, even flipping the pages of the books. The watch did not appear. Mr. Naido shook his head in disgust and began gathering up the papers and books. I saw him fold the morning newspaper and put it among the books and the loose papers. He then dusted off Ko's shoes and carefully put everything back into my rucksack.

I was furious when the principal took me to the nurse's room and had the nurse strip me naked to look for the missing watch. I gritted my teeth at this insult. There was no heat in the nurse's room. I was shivering in the late-November chill.

While putting my clothes back on I pitied myself. I wondered which was worse. Walking on the bombshell? The awful trek on an empty stomach? Being wounded by bombing? Or was it worse being constantly picked on by the girls in the school, accused of things I knew nothing about? And even worse, this enormous insult from the principal. Why, oh, why did Father and Mother bring me into this nasty world of misery? I did not beg them to be born. Why didn't Mother appear as a ghost and give the principal a big scare? Why didn't Father come back to me?

When the nurse left to report to the principal, I sat on the cold floor and cried aloud for the dishonor being dumped upon me. Wiping tears and blowing my nose, I firmly decided that no matter what Ko said, when the tuition ran out I would not go back to school. Enough is enough! I thought. Until then, I promised myself, no matter what others did to me, even if they stripped off my garments again and again, I would protect my precious name.

I went to the furnace room to pick up my rucksack. Mr. Naido told me he had read about the charges against Ko and me in the newspaper.

"What I do not understand is why the police had to release our names. Maybe that's why the principal had the nurse check me."

Mr. Naido was dumbfounded when he learned what had happened. Then he slowly said, "I firmly believe everything will turn out all right. This is the way that fate has been playing for you."

"Fate plays?" I exclaimed.

He nodded, and added that Hideyo, Ko, and I lived extremely well.

"Well?" I said. "We have exactly nothing." I went on to say how painful it was for me to have accusations from Junko Masuda hanging over our heads. Now even Kyoko's watch was missing. "I cannot take such insults anymore!" I cried in frustration. I took the newspaper out of my rucksack and twisted it as tightly as I could, pretending I was twisting the principal's arm. Then I threw the paper into the furnace.

"Where were you when Kyoko said her watch was missing?" asked Mr. Naido.

"Gymnasium. Second period," I said.

Mr. Naido was staring at one spot in the furnace room, but said nothing. Soon, slowly, he said, "S-s-someone was in the coal shed while I was gone. I—I found a strip of red cloth hanging from a nail on the low beam."

When I saw the cloth, I was sure it was Kyoko's. I remembered that I had noticed one of her ribbons was missing in the gymnasium. If I were right, the ribbon must be still missing. I raced to my homeroom. The moment I entered the class, I glanced at Kyoko's head. Indeed, one ribbon was gone.

Miss Asada came in. Looking serious, she announced that instead of studying we would be divided into groups to look for Kyoko's watch in the school building.

"There is no need to search, Miss Asada," said Kyoko. "We all know. It is Kawashima Yoko. I bet she plans to sell my watch to buy herself a pair of indoor slippers. She purposely threw hers in the toilet so that she can buy a name-brand pair. She comes to school in the same raggedy clothes day after day. She is absolutely *ugly*."

Now I knew Kyoko had dumped my precious slippers in the toilet. "I would rather have inner beauty than outward looks!" I yelled.

"Inner beauty?" questioned Kyoko. "Do you have it? No money to buy yourself new clothes or a pair of slippers would be the right words."

That was it! I stood up in fury. I moved toward her desk. I was about to yank her braided hair from the roots. But I was stopped by Miss Asada. I pushed my teacher away with great force. She staggered and rushed off.

Seeing my rage, Kyoko picked up her metal lunch box and aimed at me. It hit my mouth and I heard something crack. At the same time, blood dripped on the floor. I went completely mad.

I wiped off my bloody mouth with my sleeve and was just about to grab Kyoko's hair when the principal, Mr. Naido, and Miss Asada burst into the room. The principal stepped between us. He yelled at me to go back to my seat. Mr. Naido was holding the blackened, beat-up trash can he used for scooping coal.

I pressed my sore lips with my blouse sleeve to stop the bleeding. Chips from my front teeth tasted like chalk in my mouth. I pressed my swollen lips as hard as I could to stop their throbbing.

The principal asked Kyoko to describe her watch. She did.

"It is against the rules to bring valuable things to school. Why did you?" asked the principal.

"My father came home from France yesterday. He brought me the watch. I wanted to show it to my friends."

"Weren't you supposed to wear it on your wrist, then?" asked the principal.

"I put it in my purse, because I did not want to wear it during gym."

"Miss Yajima said you were late for roll call and did not participate in the exercises."

"I was late because I was looking for my watch and I was upset."

"You must have lost your watch between your homeroom and the gymnasium."

"No. I did not lose it. I am pretty sure Kawashima Yoko stole it."

"She has an alibi," said the principal. "Where did you go before you went to the gymnasium?"

"I stayed in the classroom and searched everyone's belongings," said Kyoko. "Then I went to your office to report the watch missing."

"Did you check Miss Kawashima's belongings?"

"No, sir! She hid her beggar's bag somewhere. I bet my watch is in it." She turned around and yelled at me, "Give me back my watch!"

I was shaky from my swollen lips, but I snapped back at her, "You are the one who hid your own watch in the coal shed."

"Me? I never put my foot in such a filthy place!"

"Where is your red ribbon?"

"Right on my hair!" said Kyoko as she touched one side of her braided loops.

"Where is the other one?" I asked.

"Right here," said Kyoko, touching the other side. But it was gone. She touched her head here and there as if to look for the ribbon.

Mr. Naido pulled the red ribbon out of his pocket and asked extremely slowly, "Is this yours?"

"That's r-r-right!" Kyoko mocked Mr. Naido. "G-g-give it to m-m-me."

My anger flared. She was mocking my only friend. Just then, Mr. Naido poured the coal onto the floor. Out dropped Kyoko's watch. Kyoko turned and stuck her tongue out at me.

The raging volcano that had been seething inside of me exploded. Quick as lightning I leaped at Kyoko and yanked her braided hair. She screamed. I persisted. The principal tried to separate us, but I would not let go of her hair. Everyone moved away, wide-eyed. The empty desks were bumped this way and that. Many chairs flipped over. The principal forcefully took hold of my back and pushed me away from Kyoko. She ran out to the hallway, crying aloud.

Because I was all worked up pulling Kyoko's hair when the principal separated us, there was still power left in me, and I accidentally punched his belly. "Ouch!" he gasped. I slugged him again, this time on purpose, for hurting me ever since I had come to the school.

I ran to the hallway and caught up with Kyoko. Again I yanked her hair as hard as I could, for dumping my slippers into the toilet. Kyoko's painful screams echoed down the corridor. I would not let her go. Everyone came to the hallway to watch. When she tried to escape into the spectators' group, they moved away from us. The more Kyoko tried to run away from me, the more I pulled. Soon the braids loosened and were badly tangled and wet by her tears. But I hung on.

It took the principal and two male teachers to

separate Kyoko and me. The screaming Kyoko ran away fast as she could. I stood still to catch my breath, holding strands of black hair in my trembling hands. For a while no one spoke. Everyone stood still in silence, even the principal. I glared at him as if to say, Do not make me mad anymore—I can explode. He ordered everyone back to their classrooms. Mr. Naido turned to go back to his post and gave me a large grin. He said, "Fooought well!"

As I headed slowly to the streetcar stop, I felt deep shame for losing my temper. Now my lips were swollen and my two front teeth broken. How would I tell Ko and Hideyo about my fight with Kyoko?

A shiny black taxi stopped near me. "Here she is!" yelled Kyoko. She had summoned her mother. Quickly Mrs. Sawayama got out of the taxi, and pushed me roughly back inside to the principal's office.

In front of me, Mrs. Sawayama demanded to know where her daughter's stolen watch was and why Kyoko was picked on at school all the time by that animal-like student, Kawashima Yoko. "She is extremely dangerous, plus she is a criminal! You must suspend her immediately," said Mrs. Sawayama. "Otherwise I must report this incident to the central government."

The principal told her what had happened. "Here is your daughter's watch and her ribbon," he said as he put them on his desk.

"I do not believe my daughter would cause any trouble at school," said Mrs. Sawayama. But the principal said the students and teachers would bear witness. "What are you going to do about Kawashima Yoko?" asked Mrs. Sawayama.

"Absolutely nothing. You will have to pay her dental bill. Besides, Kyoko has disobeyed the school rules, so we must suspend her for three months."

By the time I arrived at the hospital, it was completely dark. Before I went to Ko's, I entered Mrs. Minato's room to ask if she still had the morning paper. "You did not take it to Ko?" I asked. She shook her head.

"What happened to your lips?" she asked.

I told her, "I have no time to tell the whole story, but one of the girls threw her lunch box at me." I took the newspaper and tore out the section that told that Junko Masuda had charged Ko and me with crimes.

The moment I walked into Ko's room, she started asking what had gone wrong. I tried hard not to speak so that she would not notice my broken teeth. But when I gave her a sponge bath she saw the damage. I told her as much as I could, omitting the parts about Kyoko throwing my slippers into the toilet and the charges in the morning papers.

After listening, Ko said, "Wicked, sly, nasty

witch! I am glad you lost your temper! But do not explode again. Hear me?" I nodded. While I was making our supper, Ko read the paper. She complained that Mrs. Minato had a bad habit of tearing bits from the newspaper before she had a chance to read it. However, when she read the notice of a funeral service for Mr. and Mrs. Masuda, Ko said, "It will be on Friday afternoon at Myoshin Temple. You must attend to represent the Kawashima family."

Though I did not want to tell Hideyo what had happened, there was no way to hide it. "Now my mouth is sore, and I am sick to have such big chips out of my front teeth," I said.

"Out of temper, out of money! Remember that!" Hideyo said. "Let's ask Dr. Yamada if he knows a skillful dentist."

SOLVED

Hideyo wrote a note to the principal, asking permission for my early dismissal so that I could attend the funeral services for Mr. and Mrs. Masuda. Because I was not properly dressed for a funeral, I was going to sit at the rear corner of the main altar. I took Ko's shoes off at the entrance, but I froze when I heard people talking.

"We were very sorry that your aunt and uncle died in the fire," said one woman.

"They were murdered," said Junko Masuda. How could I forget the voice of the woman who shouted and threw me out into the street when a train was coming?

"How do you know they were murdered?" asked another voice.

"The police have released the suspects' names," Junko replied.

"The paper only said you have filed charges against the young Kawashima girls. That does not prove anything," said a woman with a loud voice.

"As young as they are, and walking around with men at night proves they could do anything!" said Junko. "Even killing and stealing!" Now, I knew for sure; Junko was the one who had telephoned the principal.

After that, I could not stay for the funeral service. I went out to sell Ko's handicrafts and quickly sold three bibs. I was motivated. Soon I found myself on the same road where I had met the old man with the daikon greens. I searched for him in the field. He was there, adding compost to the soil. I called loudly to get his attention. He stretched his back and put his shaky hand behind his ear to hear better. "Do you remember me?" I asked, approaching him.

"I do," said the old man bluntly.

I told him I had wanted to leave him a note of thanks for his kindness when Brother and I picked up the greens, but I had not had paper or pencil. "I am sorry." I presented him with an apron to give to his wife.

"No need! I cannot read," he said. "Did you come here to work, or what? Don't waste my time."

"Do you have work for me?" I asked, surprised. Yes, he said, but he would have to pay me with old rice, dry soybeans, and vegetables, for he had no cash. My whole inside jumped with joy. I could cook some rice for my family tonight and save the rest for the New Year's celebration. I would use some of the beans to make beanbag toys.

I had to spread compost on the field. The old man said, "Do just a couple of rows this afternoon, and come back tomorrow and the next day to finish." For the first time I introduced myself. I asked his name. He was Mr. Maki. He told me to walk with him to his home so that he could pay me. While walking I told him all that had happened since the day we met.

"You have no parents?" he yelled, and stared at me.

I said, "We have Father, but we do not know where he is. I know he will return to us. He must!"

For the next two days I went back to Mr. Maki's field. We piled the compost onto his cart and spread it along the rows. I was exhausted when I finished, but I earned more rice and vegetables.

Before going home that evening, I wanted to

stop by the bank of the stream near the old ware-house to gather wood scraps for fuel. I took a shortcut. Along the way I saw a long maple branch broken from a tree and about to fall to the ground. I yanked it and snipped off the leaves to make a long stick, thinking it would make fuel when cut into small pieces. I saved the some of the leaves. They would make excellent decorations.

I came to the area where I had lost sight of Goro. In front of the packed slum ran the smelly open gutter. I stood and gazed at it for a while. Suddenly I remembered that when Hideyo and I had gone to Dr. Yamada's shed a few days after the fire, Hideyo had followed Morita because his boots were wet. When he returned, he told the doctor that Morita had put his feet in the gutter and stamped in the water. So I put my stick deep into the water and dragged it as I walked.

Clink! The stick stopped. I stopped, walked back a few steps, and carefully dragged the stick again. *Clink!* I poked at the clinking spot and felt a large, hard object. I dragged the stick again and started to walk forward. The stick bumped into something else. I stopped. Again I walked back a few steps and slowly dragged the stick along. There is something down there, I thought. It's small, but long.

I ran to Dr. Yamada's office. The rucksack filled with rice and vegetables bounced on my back and I dragged my long stick on the dirt road. I asked Mrs. Yamada to telephone the police station to see if Sergeant Kudo was on duty. She was told he was on the midnight shift.

I could scarcely wait until I was alone with Hideyo at the hospital sink, to tell him about my discovery.

"After Ko goes to sleep, let us go there," I said.

"You stay!" Hideyo said.

I shook my head firmly. "I just have to find out what's in the gutter!"

Hideyo went to the public telephone to tell Dr. Yamada we would be at his house around ten-thirty that evening and to please relay the message to Sergeant Kudo.

When we got to Dr. Yamada's house, Sergeant Kudo told us that there had been no fireworks permit issued in the area since last summer. That meant Morita had lied to the doctor about how he had injured his left cheek. Sergeant Kudo was almost sure Morita was the killer.

We were ready to set out for the gutter. Mrs. Yamada, who was also curious, wanted to go with us. "We should not walk together," said Sergeant Kudo.

The doctor sprinkled a small portion of sake on Hideyo's head and shoulders and said, "This should fool everybody." So Hideyo acted drunk, staggering and singing as he took off with my long maple stick. Mrs. Yamada and I acted as though we had just finished bathing at a public bathhouse. We each carried a small bath pan and a towel. We walked slowly toward the gutter. Dr.

Yamada carried his black bag, as if he were making a house call. Sergeant Kudo was dressed like a bum, but underneath his shabby clothes he wore his police uniform. A faint glow from a streetlamp gave us enough light.

Hideyo looked like a real drunkard. He put his legs in the smelly sewer, loudly singing nursery songs in Japanese while searching for the clinking object. Mrs. Yamada and I stood not too far from Hideyo, watching. Sergeant Kudo and Doctor Yamada hid themselves in the shadows of a corner house.

Hideyo's melody was the same, but he suddenly switched the wording to Korean. He was giving me an important message. "I have found, I have found a treasure box. Go get help, get help, do not waste any time." Then Hideyo gave a big burp and sat at the edge of the gutter, with his body twisting around from side to side to search for another object near his foot. He kept on humming. Soon he sang in Korean, "I have found, I have found a broadax. Get help, get help, do not waste any time."

I ran to tell Dr. Yamada and Sergeant Kudo what Hideyo had found. They both came to the gutter. Sergeant Kudo stuck in his hand and pulled out the clinking object. It was the cash box! I had seen it several times before when Mrs. Masuda carried it from the factory to their home. Sergeant Kudo put it back in the gutter. Hideyo whispered to the sergeant about the broadax. The Sergeant pulled out the broadax. Dr. Yamada witnessed this and the sergeant returned the ax to the gutter. It must have been the weapon that killed Mr. and Mrs. Masuda. I stood there speechless!

"Hey! You! Scram! Now!" screamed a man's voice. He was running toward the gutter. "Get the hell out of there!" He was a short, stout, and slightly hunchbacked man. He had a small patch on the left side of his face. Morita, I thought. He suddenly realized that Dr. Yamada and Sergeant Kudo were kneeling by Hideyo.

"Oh! Doc, what are you doing here this time of the night?" asked Morita. The doctor said he had been on his way home from a house call when he saw a drunken man falling into the gutter. "We are trying to pull him out, but he weighs tons! Pitch in and help, Morita."

Hideyo was pulled out. They helped him stand. Hideyo's body was swaying. "Thanks," he slurred, showing a drunken smile. As he was staggering, he sang loudly in Korean, "I shall meet you at the doctor's." Sergeant Kudo quickly walked off, passed Hideyo, and vanished into the darkness. Hideyo was singing louder than ever in Korean, "He passed me, he passed me to call his big boss!"

"Lousy Korean!" said Morita. "The government should not allow them to stay in our country."

Dr. Yamada picked up his black bag. "Good night," he said. We left the scene quickly.

Hideyo was waiting at the doctor's house. He had already washed himself at a pump by the shed. Sergeant Kudo had telephoned police headquarters, explained, and gone back to the gutter to watch. Dr. Yamada also telephoned the police chief. "Send some aid for surveillance right away. Morita is a strong man. I am afraid Sergeant Kudo cannot handle this alone, especially if Goro shows up."

Later, Hideyo and I sat in front of the police chief. He thanked us for our cooperation in helping them arrest the culprits: Morita, Goro, and Junko Masuda. "It's November twenty-ninth, today," said the police chief, looking toward the wall calendar. "It took us sixty-four days to solve the case. Not bad!"

"To me it was like six hundred and forty years!" I said. Hideyo agreed with a deep nod.

"How did you guess Junko Masuda had something to do with this?" I asked.

"The way she sent in the insurance claim," said the police chief. "Junko Masuda listed the cause of the fire as 'tenant carelessness.' Then the company asked the police department to verify the cause of the fire. We knew it was not from your carelessness."

"But you did not have to release Ko's and my names to the newspapers," I said. "Because of that I was accused of stealing a girl's watch in my school. I was angry." I remembered how the nurse had stripped me naked to look for Kyoko's watch.

"It was done purposely to make the criminals relax so we could catch them more quickly. I am sorry about it." The police chief smiled and told us that the three culprits had planned the crime, but Junko Masuda did not know Goro and Morita had stolen the cash box from the factory. So she believed Ko and I had stolen it when the fire broke out.

"Now I know why she threw me on the street," I said. "But she did know I had nothing to do with the fire. Why did she scream at me that I killed her aunty and uncle and set the fire?"

"To make everybody believe you did it," said the police chief. He told us that Goro and Morita were relatives of Mr. Masuda. Goro was once the manager of the clog factory, but Mr. and Mrs. Masuda had fired him because he was lazy and a cheat. Factory workers told the police that Goro had come back to the factory many times, asking for his old job. Mr. and Mrs. Masuda would not listen to him. Goro became vindictive.

Junko had been angry with her elderly aunt and uncle ever since she'd learned that she was not their heir. All of their money and property were going to go to the Handicapped Children's Home in Tokyo. She knew Goro wanted to get even with her uncle and aunt after being fired from the factory. So she made a proposal to Goro. If he would burn the factory, especially the office where her uncle and aunt kept their will, she would pay him handsomely. She figured that without the will she would eventually receive everything from their large fire-insurance policy because she was the next of kin.

Goro knew the Masudas went to Tokyo periodically on weekends. He planned to burn the factory during one of those weekends, just about the time we were cooking our supper. That way we could be blamed for it. He asked Morita to help him.

On the Sunday evening in late September when I had spotted Goro walking between the factory and the warehouse, he was looking for a way to enter the factory. The entrance-door lock had been changed since he'd been fired, but he knew where the cash box was hidden.

Morita was going to help set the blaze. He was waiting by the outhouse for a signal from Goro. When Ko came out unexpectedly and poked his face with her stick, the robbers retreated. Morita went back home to treat the burn. (He did not go to Dr. Yamada's office until the next day.)

The robbers did not go back to the factory until sometime after 12:30 A.M. They thought the Masudas, tired by their trip, would be sound asleep at that hour. This time Goro carried a broadax to break down the door, but it was unlocked. Mr. Masuda was inside counting out Friday's and Saturday's sales receipts and handing the money to his wife. She was putting it away in the cash box. When the robbers demanded the money, she refused to give them the cash box. Goro gave Mrs. Masuda a powerful blow and forcefully took the box away from her. Mr. Masuda, who was handicapped, struggled to get up to protect his wife. Morita knocked him flat, and Goro struck Mr. Masuda on the back of his head with the broadax.

Morita splashed kerosene around. Angered and frightened, Mrs. Masuda charged fiercely at Goro. She scratched his face and neck in many places. (Sergeant Kudo said the laboratory test confirmed that the skin particles in Mrs. Masuda's fingernails matched the skin from Goro's neck.) The fire leaped here and there. An ember burned Goro's neck. Mrs. Masuda, coughing in the smoke, chased Goro to get the cash box back, but he struck her forehead with the broadax. Then the two culprits left the scene.

After the crime, Goro and Morita thought the gutter would be a safe place to hide the murder weapon and the cash box for themselves.

All the next day, I was ecstatic about our names being cleared. While preparing supper I even hummed "Home Sweet Home." I was giving Ko a sponge bath when Mrs. Minato brought in the evening newspaper. She was smiling. "You forgot this!" she said. While waiting for Hideyo, Ko read the paper and learned everything.

"You are dumb, Little One," she said. "Why

didn't you tell me what was going on?"

"I did not want you to worry. I was afraid it would slow your recovery."

"You are absolutely Stupid One!" said Ko, folding the paper with her good hand, but she did not sound as if she were really putting me down.

"If you share your worries with me, it will be only half the burden on your back," said Ko, smiling. "If you share your joy, it will make us doubly joyful. Remember that!"

PART TWO

WAS FATHER KILLED?

A little over two months had passed since Ko's accident, but the swelling hadn't gone completely from her face. There were still dark brownish spots around her eyes and cheeks. When I got home from school, Ko told me that the nurse had wheeled her to the X-ray room that morning. The chief surgeon discovered there was a silk-thread-like crack on her hip. However, he called it minor, when compared to the damage to her legs. He urged Ko to take calcium tablets twice a day. She asked him when he would release her.

"When I am ready," said the surgeon.

Ko was distressed. "It's easy for the doctor to answer like that, but how about my feelings? The longer I stay, the more the bill piles up!" Ko complained about it to Hideyo as soon as he came in.

"The surgeon is right," said Hideyo. "Your responsibility is to get well fast."

"I have so much on my mind," said Ko. "I am not allowed to sit up in bed yet. At least if I could sit up, I could sew a blouse for our Little One. The New Year is a month away." Ko choked up in tears.

"Crying is not going to get you anywhere," said Hideyo in a low voice, just as Father used to talk when he was serious. "Remember, for today, today's wind blows, and for tomorrow, tomorrow's wind blows. Why do you worry when you cannot do much? Where is your patience?"

"Gone for good!" said Ko in defiance.

Just then an evening nurse came in to check on Ko. She said to Hideyo, "The hospital administrator wishes to see you in the office as soon as possible."

"It's about paying the bill, I bet!" Ko exclaimed.

The nurse then handed me a package. "This is for you," she said.

"A package from Corporal Matsumura!" I was excited and sat right on the floor to open it. He had sent us a large package of dried seaweed and several stamps. I read his note aloud:

"I WAS EXTREMELY SORRY TO HEAR OF THE MISHAP WITH SISTER KO. MY WIFE AND I WISH HER A SPEEDY RECOVERY. IT IS MY GREAT REGRET THAT I COULD NOT BE THERE NOW. MY WIFE HAD A DIFFICULT PREGNANCY AND SHE LOST OUR FIRST MAN-CHILD. SHE HAS NOT BEEN WELL EVER SINCE. BESIDES LOOKING AFTER MY WIFE, I HAVE BEEN TRYING TO REBUILD OUR DEMOLISHED TEXTILE COMPANY. AS SOON AS WE ARE SETTLED, I SHALL VISIT YOU. I AM STILL SENDING YOUR FATHER'S NAME TO THE NATIONWIDE RADIO SHOW CALLED, 'SEARCH FOR PERSONS.' HOLD ON, LITTLE FRIEND, UNTIL YOUR

HONORABLE FATHER'S RETURN, AND KEEP
ON SENDING ME NEWS OF SISTER KO'S
PROGRESS. GREETINGS TO BROTHER.

CORPORAL MATSUMURA

Hideyo entered the room as I finished writing a
letter of thanks to the corporal. The hospital
administrator had told him that patients must
pay their bill on the third day of every month.

"I have been here over two months," said Ko,
worrying. "How can we pay?"

"Why don't you shut up and listen to me,"
said Hideyo. "That's the trouble with you girls!"

Hideyo said that while talking to the hospital
administrator about making some arrangement
to pay the bill, he had learned that a night
watchman at the university hospital had retired.
They were looking for a young man, preferably
one who knew the martial arts. The hours were
from 6:00 P.M. to midnight, seven days a week.
Hideyo had said he wanted the job. When he
told the administrator how he had caught the
robber, he was hired. His entire salary would go
to pay the hospital bill. "But for the first pay-
ment I must use all the wrapping-cloth money."

"No!" Ko shook her head. "It is for an
emergency!"

"If this is not an emergency, then what is?" I
snapped.

"Look! Sister! I am the head of the family. You must obey me!" Hideyo said firmly. "As long as we have our health, we can gain back the money."

Hideyo assured us that working the midshift hours seven days a week would pay him well. Also, as long as he worked for the university hospital, he would have the privilege of borrowing books from the library. Hideyo planned to read to prepare himself to enter the university in the future. "It will be difficult, but let us cooperate until Father's return."

"When will you start work as a night watchman?" I asked Hideyo.

"Tomorrow. On the first of December."

"Laboring all day on the cold streets, then going to work again until midnight!" said Ko, feeling bad for Hideyo. "It will be extremely hard for you."

"No!" Hideyo shook his head. "Nothing is hard compared to my escape from Nanam."

When Hideyo mentioned the word *escape*, my thoughts turned like a revolving lantern on the scenes of that horrifying time. I shuddered. Ko's eyes gazed at the stained ceiling and her lips tightened. I wanted to escape from the memories.

"Will you teach me how to make aprons?" I asked Ko. "The New Year's holiday is coming, and I might be able to sell some. I also want to make more beanbag toys. I saved soybeans for that." We had some good material from the patients' discarded bedclothes.

"Tomorrow," murmured Ko, her eyes still gazing at the ceiling. "Because of me, we have to use up the wrapping-cloth money! I am disastrous."

"I am glad you are disastrous," said Hideyo, smiling. "Remember the old saying, 'After three years, even disaster can prove a blessing!' So get well!"

Hideyo would come home from his day job looking cold, tired, and hungry. But there was no time for him to relax. After a few moments with us, he would re-wrap himself in his blanket and go out to check the hospital security on his first round. It took him about two and a half to three hours to make one round, so I had enough time to take care of both Ko and Mrs. Minato before Hideyo got back.

I looked forward to Hideyo's thirty-minute supper break. "How do you like your new work?" I asked, remembering our dinner gatherings in the bamboo grove. Father always wanted to know how we were doing.

Hideyo said, "The watchman's job is not very strenuous or dangerous. However, there is lots of responsibility. I have to be sure everything is safe and sound."

"What do you mean, not dangerous?" I asked.

"During my day job, at lunch hour, two laborers began arguing, and that led to fistfighting. One threw his pick at the other. The pick almost hit me, so I ran to the neighboring police post for help. By the time I got back with the policeman, the second laborer's stomach was burst open and he was dead. Both of them were stupid!" said Hideyo. "There is no winner in fighting."

"That goes for war also. War is stupid!" Ko said. "I wonder, just when are people going to realize it?"

"Did the man who was killed have a family?" I asked.

Hideyo said, "He was married with two small boys."

When Hideyo took off for his second round, I finished my homework. Then I washed our underwear at the wooden sink, thinking of the dead man's two little boys. They needed their father, just as I needed mine . . . but I could still believe my father would join us one day.

Because the surgeon said Ko needed calcium, I stopped at the fish market on my way home from school. A middle-aged woman in a black rubber apron was filleting cods and throwing the skeletons into a wooden tub. I asked the woman if I might have one. "Help yourself," she said, continuing her work. I chose the largest one. The head was still attached to the skeleton.

We will have a good soup for the next couple of days and more calcium for Ko, I thought, grinning in my heart. I held the fish by its mouth and headed for the hospital with a happy skip in my step. The skeleton flipped and flopped here and there beside me.

Suddenly, fishy-smelling cold water splashed over me. Slimy water full of scales dripped down my face. Right behind me stood Sumiko, Kyoko's best friend, holding a bucket. "I got you now! You troublemaker! Don't you ever come around our fish market to beg again!" Sumiko sneered.

I almost slapped her with the fish skeleton, but knowing Ko needed it, I ran as fast as I could to get away from Sumiko. My blouse and skirt stuck to me, and the winter wind made me shiver.

Ko did not know whether to laugh or fume when I stood in front of her in my dripping-wet, smelly, scale-covered clothes, clutching my ruck-sack and the skeleton of a codfish. "What happened?" she asked. I told her I was accidentally sprayed with water at the fish market.

Though Ko's room did not have heat, I took a sponge bath right away. Then I washed my hair and my smelly clothes at the sink. When I returned, Ko's face was extremely pale and she was breathing heavily. The newspaper was scattered on the floor. Mrs. Minato must have brought it.

"What's wrong?" I asked, panicking.

"Water," she begged, running her tongue over her lips. Quickly I brought her a wooden soup bowl half filled, for I thought she was going to die. I remembered Mother asking for water in the Kyoto train station before she left us for good. Ko raised her head and drank the water. Then she dropped her head back down onto the pillow. Her lips were quivering and her breathing was rough.

"Hold on! I will go get a nurse!" I cried. She shook her head.

"Little One, Father may be dead!" Ko said, biting her lips and trying hard to stop trembling. She pointed to the newspapers.

I read that Mr. Yoshida, the prime minister, was negotiating with the Soviet government for the release of the remaining Japanese prisoners. The newspaper said the Kremlin had announced that farmers and working-class civilians would be released within a month. The remaining prisoners would be put on trial and, if found guilty as charged, they would be executed as war criminals. Father would be one of these people because of his high ranking. There were long lists, in alphabetical order, of the prisoners' names. Trying hard not to cry, I earnestly went through to find Father's name, but Kawashima Yoshio was not there. My tears blurred the print on the newspaper.

"The Russians must have killed Father right after they captured him!" Ko said in a faint but sorrowful voice.

When Ko said the word *killed*, my memory went back to the day when we were caught in Korea by the Communist soldiers, who pointed guns at us. Did the Russians kill Father that way? My knees shook, my heart raced, and I felt like fainting.

"I do not trust the Kremlin," said Ko, sniffling.

Was Father dead? I wanted to scream and smash the windowpane with my fist, but I felt weak. I cannot faint now! I said to myself. If I did, I feared Ko might die! I did not want her to see me this way. I slowly sat on the floor, and crawled under her bed to lie down. I closed my eyes, took a deep breath, and whispered in my heart, Father, stay alive!

"Maybe Father disguised himself as a farmer, and that's why his name was not listed," I said.

"Good try," Ko said weakly. "Father would never cheat. He is a man of honesty and justice."

"I am sure the Russians would let our government know if they had executed Father!" I said. "Because of his position."

Ko shook her head. "They are sly, cunning, and secretive! They are devils!"

Hideyo came home from his day job. His cheeks were red. "It's snowing," he said, unwrapping himself from his blanket. When our eyes met, Hideyo gave me a look that said, What's going on? I handed him a bowl of hot fish broth. While he was sipping, his eyes went back and forth between Ko and me. He must have thought I had argued with her, but he did not have time to talk. "See you later. Behave, Little One!" he said, taking his blanket and disappearing into the darkness to make his rounds.

While waiting for Hideyo's break, I began sewing aprons under Ko's direction. If I made one stitch bigger than another, she told me to do it over again. "Put your heart and soul into the sewing. The finishing should be beautiful."

"If I make such fine stitches, I will never finish!"

"No one wants to buy a sloppily stitched apron," Ko said firmly.

I obeyed Ko, but I had Father on my mind now. The more I thought of Father, the more my hands would not behave. I could not concentrate on the stitches.

"I am starved!" Hideyo said as he came in from the first round, wiping his frosty eyeglasses. He sat in front of the apple-box table and began to sip his fish soup, sucking the bones.

"It's awfully quiet here," said Hideyo. "Were you two fighting again? Come clean." When I handed him the newspaper, he stopped eating. His eyes were glued to the page for several minutes. But when he finished reading, he calmly raised his head and asked, "Is there more soup? This is delicious."

I thought the news would disturb Hideyo. Instead he asked how my day had gone at school and if I was keeping up with all my subjects. My brother irritated me. He never showed any sign of worry or anger. "Aren't you worried about Father?"

"No! Unless I see Father's official death certificate and his belongings with my own eyes, I refuse to think he has died." Hideyo bit his lips and his face muscles tightened as he looked at me. I wished he would throw a few curses into the air to release his tension.

I began sewing the apron again. Ko put a paperback book on her chest. Holding the pages with her left hand, she began to read. Often she would stare at the ceiling and make a depressing sigh. She could not concentrate on the book either, for her mind, like mine, was filled with Father. "You should go to bed now," she said.

"I want to finish sewing," I told her. "Tomorrow is Saturday—no school in the afternoon. I want to sell this apron if I can, along with some kimonos for babies."

At school everyone was excited and talking about how they were going to spend the New Year's holiday. Some were going skiing in the north, some were going to the hot spring near Mount Fuji, and some were going on a sightseeing tour south of Honshu. I knew I would be making the trip to Maizuru, where boats brought the refugees, to paste Father's name poster on the wall.

On my way to biology class, I caught sight of the daily bulletin board. There was a large drawing of me gripping a codfish skeleton. The caption read, GUESS WHO? I was hurt and mad. What do the other girls know about being hungry, homeless, and missing someone they love so much? As I looked at the drawing, I wanted to yank it down. Then, standing there, I suddenly realized that in spite of our cruel condition, Hideyo, Ko, and I were helping one another live day by day. We kept the hope of Father's return alive. I had absolutely nothing material, but I had a brother and a sister who gave me their love. They were teaching me the value of human life. We had not done anything to be ashamed of. I was proud of what we'd been doing. How petty of the girls who saw the drawing and made fun of me! I decided then to leave it there. The more they made fun of me, the more stubbornly I would show them my serenity.

Mr. Iwai, the biology teacher, noticed the drawing as he passed, carrying a large box. He gave me a compassionate look and put the box down so that he could reach to remove the drawing. But I asked him not to. "It is a beautiful drawing," I said. "Let everyone admire it." He gave me a mystified look.

"Have you seen hatched silkworms before?" he asked.

"No, sir."

He opened the box and showed me many tiny silkworms vigorously eating mulberry leaves.

"I am looking for someone to do a report on them and exhibit the research at the city science fair," he said. "Would you like to do it?"

"You mean, to watch the worms grow, and

describe their creation of cocoons, and their transformation from pupa to moth . . . until finally they lay eggs and die?"

"Right, but one more thing," said Mr. Iwai. "You must cook the cocoons and spin silk thread to complete the project."

"Thank you, sir. But I have no room at home to keep them," I said. "I have no thread spinner."

"Use the biology laboratory until the worms are ready to make cocoons," said Mr. Iwai, handing me the box. "I will find you the spinner."

After school, I headed for town with my newly sewn apron and the baby kimonos and bibs Ko had finished before her accident. I stopped at a cozy-looking house surrounded by a camellia hedge. After the lady of the house looked at the apron, flipping it inside out to examine the stitches, she bought it. I was glad. A baby started crying. "Do you have a newborn?" I asked. She said she had a little baby boy.

"Congratulations!" I bowed, and quickly pulled out a bib. "I would like to present this bib to your baby." She was surprised at my gift. Her baby was crying harder now. The lady left for a few moments and came back with the boy-child in her arms. "Oh, baby! You are wet! You wet all the time," she said. "I just changed you and I have no more kimonos for you."

"Are you interested in a kimono?" I asked.

"Do you sell them, too?" She was surprised.

I wished hard that she would buy one. I

wanted to get toothbrushes and a tube of tooth-paste for Hideyo, Ko, and me for New Year's. I showed her three soft flannel kimonos from my wrapping cloth.

This time she did not examine stitches. "Who made these?" asked the lady.

"My sister," I answered.

"Beautiful work," she said. "Give me all you have!" I could not believe my ears. She wanted them all!

She asked me if I had four more aprons to sell. She wanted to give them as New Year's presents to her mother and three sisters. I said, "I will make the aprons and deliver them before the holiday." I was excited. I took her name and address and introduced myself. She was Mrs. Suzuki.

Holding my earnings tightly, I stopped at the drugstore near the hospital. After buying three toothbrushes and a tube of toothpaste, there was still some money left. I asked the druggist how much a bottle of calcium pills would cost. I counted the money, but did not have enough. I stood there for a while thinking, Which is the most important thing now? Toothbrushes and tooth-paste, or a bottle of calcium pills for Ko? I went to the druggist and said, "I changed my mind. I want to buy a bottle of calcium tablets instead."

As I returned to the hospital, it was com-pletely dark and the winter wind was biting, but the happiness of the day made me warm inside. "Where have you been all this time?" questioned

Ko, worried. "You should be home before dark!"

"The sun goes to sleep quickly in the winter." I smiled. "I have something for you!" I opened the lid of the calcium bottle and told her to open her mouth. She wanted to know why. I showed her the bottle.

"A bottle of calcium? Where did you get it?" I told her about the sale I made and that I had to make four aprons by New Year's Eve. I had two weeks to fill the order.

"Take the bottle back to the drugstore. Calcium is expensive," said Ko.

"Too late! I already opened it."

"You must learn how to manage money. You just cannot spend every yen you earn," Ko said. "You were saving for a pair of shoes. You do dumb things sometimes!"

I knew better than to argue with Ko. Besides, I was too happy to argue. I told her I would manage my earnings better next time. "Now, take this tablet, Honorable Sister. You will heal much faster. Then you can help me sew." I brought her some water. She slowly swallowed a tablet and turned her head toward the wall and sobbed.

"Why are you crying? You should be happy!"

Ko said she had just remembered that hot day of the bombing, when we were fleeing from Nanam to Seoul, when she shouted at me that she wished I were dead.

"I remember," I said. "But I was complaining all the time about my pain, deafness, thirst, and shaven head. I deserved your words."

"I really did not mean it." Ko's words were blurred by streaming tears that wet her pillow. "I regretted it very, very much."

I wiped her face with a beat-up washcloth and said, "War makes people mean and ugly, and robs everyone's gentle heart. I knew you did not mean it."

SILKWORMS

Now it was December twenty-first. In five more days school was going to let out for the New Year's holiday vacation, and I wanted to take the silkworms home so that I could continue to observe their progress. They had become transparently whitish and ready to make cocoons. I must make room for the worms under Ko's bed somehow! I thought.

When I went to the biology laboratory to pick up the silkworms, I could not find my journal or my biology assignment with the silkworm drawings. Because the journal was written on the back of trash papers, I thought the cleaning students might have mistaken them for trash. But the papers were not in the furnace room. I searched the laboratory and kept on searching until the weekly duty teacher entered and asked what I was doing. I explained that my notes were missing.

"I always leave my journal by the worm box, and a ruler was on top of the papers," I said. The ruler was to measure the worms' growth. I was frustrated. The weekly duty teacher helped me look here and there, with no luck. I carried the worm box to the furnace room to get my rucksack. On my way there, I stopped at the teachers' room to find out which team was assigned to do the laboratory cleaning. It was Sumiko's. Ever since Kyoko's suspension, Sumiko had done spiteful things to me. She had done them with more skill and daring than the other members of Kyoko's clique, and had won much admiration from the girls.

I put the silkworms into a larger box that Mr. Naido had saved for me, and asked him to check all papers before burning them. "My silkworm journal and my biology-assignment papers are missing," I said, trying very hard to control my anger.

"The girls, I bet!" Mr. Naido shouted.

Strong winds from Atago Mountain shook the furnace room, and a razor-sharp draft hit my bare arms. "H-h-high wind. I—I must not burn the trash." No one appreciated his carefulness and all the things he did for the school, but I knew Father would.

My thoughts catapulted to Father. Missing him so much brought tears to my eyes. How could he keep warm in Manchuria's severe winter? I crumpled a trash paper and blew my nose as hard as I could.

"D-d-don't cry," Mr. Naido said. "I w-will find the journal and papers for you!"

I wanted to tell him I was crying for my missing father, not the papers, but I only sniffled harder. I also wanted to tell Mr. Naido how grateful I was to him, but I could not utter a word. I took a deep breath to control myself and said in normal voice, "I do appreciate your friendship." I bowed deeply. I had completely forgotten to speak to him slowly. When I lifted up my head, tears were running down Mr. Naido's soot-covered, wrinkled face. He was smiling at me. He then looked me straight in the eye, took a huge breath, and said ever so smoothly, slowly, and clearly, "You are very, very welcome, young maiden!"

I had never heard him speak so well! I was astonished, and stared at him for a few moments. He took another deep breath, and said slowly and smoothly, "My! We have discovered something! Before we speak, we must breathe deeply; then we will have no trouble with our speech!" If he believes that by taking a deep breath before talking he can speak smoothly, then I must do just the same, I thought. I nodded and gave him a huge smile of congratulation. Again he breathed deeply and said, without any trouble, but slowly, "You look prettier when you smile. Keep on smiling."

While riding the streetcar to the hospital, I was light with happiness. I no longer minded that someone had stolen my important papers. After all, going to the furnace room to pick up a box and asking Mr. Naido to look for my papers had led him to take a deep breath before speaking. I must appreciate the loss of my papers as a piece of luck!

I took a peek at the worms. They were very ugly. Still, they had accepted their burden and lived as best they could. From the worms would come beautiful, strong, pure white threads!

Will I be a beautiful person if I, too, accept and endure burdens and go through life calmly? I wondered. If a silkworm can, then I, as a human being, certainly can! Maybe I could not be as pure and beautiful as a silk thread, but I could be like the humble wildflowers that grew along the stream bank during the spring, summer, and fall. If tramped on, they would always spring back, and give a bit of pleasure to the passersby. Suddenly I felt I had grown up. I realized how stupid I had been to be irritated by the girls.

I burst into Ko's room to tell her my new philosophy. Her bed was empty. What's wrong? I asked myself. Did she fall out of the bed? I rushed to the nurses' station and learned that Ko had been taken to the X-ray room. "Your sister will be there for a while," said a nurse. She also told me that Mrs. Minato had gone home. I was to clean up her room as quickly as possible. Another patient was already waiting.

Mrs. Minato had left me a note. She must have scribbled it quickly.

MISS YOKO. I DID NOT WANT TO CRY, SO I LEFT BEFORE YOU GOT BACK FROM SCHOOL. WHATEVER I HAVE LEFT HERE BELONGS TO THE KAWASHIMAS NOW. PLEASE TIDY UP THE ROOM. HERE IS MY ADDRESS. DO COME TO SEE ME WHENEVER YOU CAN. THANK YOU MANY TIMES FOR YOUR FAITHFUL HELP. I HAVE RECOVERED FASTER BECAUSE OF YOU! PLEASE SAY GOOD-BYE TO YOUR HONORABLE BROTHER. OH, YES, I TOLD THE NEWSPAPER MAN TO BRING THE PAPER TO YOUR SISTER'S ROOM.

SAYONARA, MRS. MINATO.

As I looked around the room, I realized she had left everything she had used—even the teakettle resting on her own shichirin and her yellow bed clothes. There were still bits of hot charcoal in the shichirin, and the teakettle was warm. I felt a sense of great loss and absentmindly stood there for a while. Then the nurse came and reminded me to get done with the cleaning.

I went back and forth between Ko's and Mrs. Minato's rooms, bringing everything she had left for us. I cleaned her room and her portion of the corridor extra carefully to welcome the new patient.

While I stood looking for a place to put Mrs.

Minato's things, two nurses wheeled Ko back into the room. Ko said, "Mrs. Minato came to say farewell, but she did not stay long, nor did she speak about leaving her belongings." I gave her Mrs. Minato's note.

"How kind!" said Ko. "When you make Brother's bed tonight, put Mrs. Minato's futon beneath his. Someday I will take apart her futon and make a fresh one for Father."

I showed Ko the silkworms. "All I have to do is prepare a box with lots of cubicle frames and watch them." I smiled. I went on to tell about Mr. Naido's speech! Ko did not say anything, but her eyes were fixed on the worm box.

"Are you listening to me?" I asked.

"About your worms—they would not crawl out and climb all over the place, would they?"

"If they do, then what?" I teased. Then I remembered that Ko did not like worms. Long ago in Nanam, Hideyo and his friends had scared her by packing night crawlers in her pencil box.

"I don't want them to crawl all over me! I can't run away from them! Nor I can shoo them away! You will have to make a tight lid."

"They will be smothered to death!" I said. I picked up the biggest worm, put it on my palm, and brought it close to Ko.

"Stay away from me!" said Ko, making a sour face.

"She would not hurt you," I said, bringing my palm near Ko's chest.

"Little One!" she said. "If you put that worm on me, I won't make you any more clothing for rest of your life!"

"Is that a promise or a threat?" I giggled.

"*Promise!* Put her back in the box. She is all yours!"

Hideyo walked in. Ko asked him, "Could those worms crawl out during the night? I do not want them to creep all over me."

"They are the best crawlers. Especially at night around people!" Hideyo teased, until he remembered the pencil-box incident. Seeing Ko's nervous face, he changed his tone and explained that the worms could not crawl out of the box. "Rest easy." Hideyo laughed.

Ko gave a sigh of relief. Then, turning to me, she asked, "Did you have some news about Mr. Naido's speech?" I told both Ko and Hideyo that Mr. Naido now could speak without any trouble. They were delighted.

Though the school closed for the New Year's holiday, I got up as early as always and worked on Mrs. Suzuki's aprons between my chores. With the leftover material, I made six beanbag toys. I delivered the aprons and I gave Mrs. Suzuki's baby a beanbag that had a tiny bell inside. She asked if I had more. I said, "I have five." She wanted them all. "These are just the right presents for my nieces," she said. "I have been so busy with my baby, I haven't had time for New Year's shopping."

She asked if Ko would make her son's name-day–blessing kimono, saying, "I do admire her stitches."

I explained Ko's situation but said, "I am certain she can do it." I figured Mrs. Suzuki's son would have to be one hundred days old or older for his name-day blessing. Surely Ko would be able to sit up by then and do a little sewing. If she could not, I wanted to make the little boy's important kimono. I asked her to buy material she liked and also matching thread. I gave her the hospital address so that she could let me know when to come and get her purchases.

A special kimono order for Mrs. Suzuki's son for his name day! I felt all bubbly as I headed back to the hospital. Now I could buy tooth-brushes and a tube of toothpaste for all of us! I'd get miso and tofu for our New Year's supper.

While serving hot water to Ko, I told her she had an important and honorable task: to sew a man-child's kimono for his name-day blessing. Ko had been exercising her good arm more and more. Her cast-covered right arm was resting over the folded hospital blanket. "I am trying to get better," she said. "So I can earn."

That evening, I made more beanbags. I asked Ko if I might go to Maizuru to sell them. While I was there I wanted to paste a poster with

Father's name on the refugee-center wall. "Just in case he is among the farmers."

"As long as you return home before dark," said Ko.

I pasted three newspapers together, wrote Father's name in huge brush writing, and added our names and the hospital address in small print on the left-hand corner.

NEW YEAR'S EVE

When I crawled out from under Ko's bed on the day of New Year's Eve, I could still see stars in the sky.

"Can't you be quiet, Little One? It's not time for me to get up," said Hideyo, half asleep.

I said I was going to the refugee center in Maizuru to sell some beanbags. "I want to come home before dark, so I have to start early."

In Ko's rucksack I carried paste in a glass jar, the newspaper poster with Father's name painted on it, and the beanbag toys. Hideyo wanted to leave with me. Because we had no overcoats, we wrapped ourselves in our own tired-looking blankets. While walking side by side, he warned me to be extra careful at the port because he had heard there were thieves there, who might attack anyone.

"I am a big girl now, and I have weapons." I smiled.

"Weapons?" Hideyo asked.

I pulled aside the blanket and showed him two long sewing needles pinned on the collar of my little red vest. Ko had made the vest from the winter coat I'd worn in Nanam. "If anyone attacks me I will poke them with needles," I said earnestly.

"They will hurt!" Hideyo laughed.

"I bet Father is cold. He left us during the summer and he has no winter jacket."

"I will write a letter to the prime minister, urging the government to search for Father. You sent a return postcard to Father's birthplace, right?" Hideyo asked.

I nodded. We had read in the recent national newspaper that every returning refugee must register at his or her birthplace. So I bought one return postcard and sent it to Aomori, asking the town officials to let Father know where we were and to let us know of Father's arrival. Such postcards cost plenty but I was determined to send one every month, even if we had to give up tofu, miso, or seaweed. It would be a great joy to receive a return postcard from the Aomori town hall!

We came to a street corner. Hideyo turned toward city hall to look for work. I went straight on to catch a train to Maizuru.

The refugee center was filled with people. There were many exhausted, hungry, sad-looking women with children, as well as begging, discharged, crippled soldiers. Many were leaning over their humble belongings, guarding their treasures. I had been like that once, I thought, and in a way I was like that still. All because of the war.

A long-haired, skinny man was sleeping under a thin, beat-up blanket on the concrete floor. Walking around barefoot was a boy, about ten, skin and bones, and pale, wearing a ragged shirt and trousers that were three sizes too large. He hugged his arms across his chest to warm himself.

As he passed the sleeping man, he quickly grabbed the blanket and ran outside. The man woke up and chased the boy, who tripped on the corner of the blanket and fell. The man caught up with the boy and began beating him. The boy shrieked for help, but, afraid of the man, no one made a move. The boy fell to the ground, screaming for help. The man grabbed the screaming boy's shoulders and banged his head on the icy ground. Blood streamed, staining the frozen earth. Then the man kicked the boy many times, picked him up in the air, and threw him to the ground as hard as he could. The boy did not cry out anymore.

"He is dead!" someone yelled. The man was breathless but glared around fiercely at the people. He squatted and unbuttoned the boy's bloody shirt and trousers and yanked them off. He spat on the naked, lifeless boy and walked off with his blanket and the boy's clothes.

Three policemen arrived on bicycles. They examined the boy and shook their heads. One policeman asked a spectator where the man had gone. The spectator pointed and described the man's looks.

The policeman took off on his bicycle at great speed. Another policeman ran into the refugee center to telephone police headquarters for an examiner, and the third stayed on as guard.

Curious people made a dense circle around the naked dead boy, peeking, whispering, and feeling sorry for him. The policeman went around the circle pushing people away, but none would go. An examiner and a few more policemen arrived with a three-wheeled cart. They examined the boy and took many pictures. Then they took the boy away in the cart.

I was glad when I saw the handcuffed long-haired killer pulled along by a policeman. I could not forgive him. Stealing was bad. But, being an adult, couldn't he have talked to the boy to teach him right from wrong, and then taken his blanket back?

I started to walk away, but one of the policemen asked me and others to identify the killer and the boy's clothes. I was scared to see the killer, but somehow I found the courage to face the situation.

As I walked to the refugee-center wall to paste up Father's name poster, I sighed sadly. The killer, the boy, and the exhausted hungry refugees, as well as my family, were the victims of World War II. "We must *never again* have war on this earth," I said to myself firmly.

I looked for a place to paste Father's name poster. Many had posted their loved ones' names. Some were written on the backs of advertisements, some were on notebook paper, some were on shoji paper, and some were on newspaper, but none were as large as mine. I saw a few faded name papers tattered and almost falling off the board. I tore them down, and pasted Father's up. I stepped back and took a look. Then I folded my hands and silently prayed, Father, come home!

I entered the refugee-center office to check the arrival list of refugees in the *Ka* section. Kawashima Yoshio was not on the list. On the request form I filled in Father's name and his birthplace and wrote down where to contact us upon his arrival from Russia or Manchuria.

On the Maizuru main street the store entrances were decorated with New Year's ornaments. I went to a toy shop and asked the shopkeeper if he would buy my beanbag toys. He shook his head. Back on the street I saw many men and women pulling their merchandise carts. Some carts were for footwear, some for clothing, some for toilet articles. Some had baskets filled with eating utensils, and some had cooked noodles. I followed them. At the shrine grounds they quickly began setting up a marketplace.

I went to the altar and prayed earnestly for Ko's speedy recovery and for Father to join us very soon. Sitting on the altar steps, I ate one of the hardened biscuits that Mrs. Minato had left for us in her room. While eating, I remembered when Ko and I had come to Maizuru to paste Hideyo's name papers. Then she had bought two hot sweet potatoes from a pushcart man and we sat on a concrete wall by the waterfront, swinging our legs, with the breeze in our hair, eating the potatoes.

People began to fill the area to do last-minute shopping. I saw a mother with young children, so I showed her my beanbags. "Will you get me a beanbag for the New Year?" begged a little girl. The mother picked up the beanbags, examined the seams by trying to pull them apart, then tossed the toys up in the air a couple of times. "Good beanbags," she said. "Sell me all of them."

Before I took the train back to Kyoto, I went to the refugee center once more, and took another look at Father's name poster on the wall. It was still there. I smiled and earnestly wished that no one would peel it from the board. Father *must* come home, I said to myself.

As soon as I got off the train I headed for the station switchyard, and picked up coal between the ties and rails. I stuffed as much as I could into Ko's rucksack. It was heavy, and at each step the lumps of coal poked my back, but I was filled with happiness to think I was now able to buy

New Year's presents for Brother and Sister.

When I got back to the hospital, Ko was cheerful. "Welcome home," she said. "You made it before sundown! Let me hear the news from the center." I said I would tell her while we ate supper, but first I had things to do.

I crawled under her bed to check the silkworms. They were making cocoons. I took all the money paid to me by Mrs. Suzuki and dashed out to the general store. Besides tofu and miso, I bought three toothbrushes and a tube of toothpaste and three freshly made traditional New Year's rice cakes, fluffy and sweet.

I hid my purchases under Ko's bed. Then I brought out Mother's ashes and put them on top of Hideyo's rolled bedding. "It's New Year's Eve. Mother should be with us," I said. "Someday we will be able to afford a real altar and flowers for her!"

Hideyo came home looking starved. He had left for work without breakfast and had had no time for lunch. "I cannot wait to hear about your trip to the refugee center," he said, rushing out for his first round.

Because Mrs. Minato had left us her shichirin, cooking was much easier and faster. We'd also inherited her rice bowls and a few small china plates. While a salted codfish head was roasting on the hospital shichirin outside the window and the rice was steaming on Mrs. Minato's shichirin inside, I bathed Ko and combed her hair. I went out onto the hospital grounds, snipped small pine and bamboo branches, tied them together, and made two bouquets—one for Mother's ashes, and the other to hang on the door of Ko's room to welcome the New Year.

While listening to the teakettle gently boiling, we had supper. How I wished we had green tea to complete this special evening. But remembering the scene at the refugee center, I realized how fortunate I was to have both Brother and Sister and to be able to sleep in peace.

When I was about to pour hot water for Ko and Hideyo, my brother pulled a tiny package from his trousers pocket. He took the lid off the teakettle and quickly poured in a small portion of tea leaves. He smiled at me, tightened his lips, and shook his head. He meant, *Hush!* I looked at Ko. Her eyes were closed as though she was appreciating the supper, and she held her empty rice bowl tightly on her chest, waiting for hot water.

"I have to leave for another round soon," Hideyo said. Reaching out for the teakettle, he poured hot green tea into Ko's rice bowl.

"This is going to be your lucky year, Sister. Happy New Year!" Hideyo greeted Ko.

Ko could not believe the steamy hot green tea. "Where did you get this?" she asked. Hideyo was silent. Ko closed her eyes and took a deep breath. "This is high-quality tea," Ko murmured. "It must be expensive. Where did you get the extra money?"

"Enjoy your tea and I will tell you," said Hideyo, filling our rice bowls.

After sipping, he began. "Remember when the two laborers fought and one was killed? On my way home that day, I found five yen on the ground. I took the money to the nearest police post, hoping someone would go there to pick it up. On my way home this evening, I passed the same police post. I stopped to see if anybody had come by for the money. The police said, 'No one has, and the money is yours.' It pays to be honest! So I splurged." He gave us a mischievous smile. "New Year comes but once a year, and we only live once, so why not indulge ourselves with good tea! Happy New Year, my sisters!"

"I will be fourteen!" I smiled as I sipped my tea.

"I sincerely thank both of you for your care," Ko said. "Happy New Year."

While Hideyo was gone for his next round, I kept the teakettle on the shichirin. The fire was low. I placed the three rice bowls on the apple-box table so that we could have more tea when Hideyo returned. I did not bring out the three plates for the rice cakes, as Ko might suspect something. I went to the drafty wooden sink and washed our supper dishes and did the laundry. I was freezing by the time I hurried back to Ko's room.

I could not believe my eyes when I got there. I almost dropped everything I was carrying. Two nurses were holding Ko under her arms, trying to sit her up on the bed!

The surgeon rolled a hospital blanket tightly and put it behind her back. "Pull her up a bit more!" said the doctor. He very carefully helped Ko lean on the blanket. One nurse put a sling on her right arm immediately. "There!" the doctor said. Ko was weak, but smiling. The doctor said to the other nurse, "Miss Ko can sit up for five minutes." Through his stethoscope he listened to Ko's heart. He took hold of Ko's injured hand and asked her to squeeze his hand as tightly as she could. He nodded and seemed satisfied.

When the doctor saw me standing there, he said, "Continue with the canteen hot-water bottles!" I chuckled because I remembered his face, when, right after Ko's surgery, he'd pulled out the canteens one after another and asked, "What are these?"

How I wished Hideyo could see this wonderful moment. Ko was able to sit! I could have jumped up and down.

"Remember, just five minutes," the doctor said firmly to the nurses as he left Ko's room. "If she feels dizzy, let her lie down immediately."

"I did not expect this surprise," Ko said. She looked exhausted, but happy.

One nurse said, "The X ray showed your hip-bone is doing well."

Ko asked her the time. She said it was eleven, and continued, "One more hour and we will have a new year."

"I wish I could sit up until midnight!" Ko said.

She was breathing rather heavily. In one more hour Hideyo would be home. I knew Ko wanted to welcome Hideyo in a sitting position.

"I am sure you want to welcome the new year sitting up, but you are not strong enough," said the nurse. Ko's eyes and mine met and we smiled, for the nurse did not understand our wishes.

The nurses said Ko must lie down. They took off the sling and rested her cast arm on the rolled blanket. A nurse hung the sling over the bedpost, saying Ko would need it whenever she sat up.

"Little One, I am going to rest now, but wake me when Honorable Brother gets home," Ko said. Sitting for only five minutes had tired her out.

While she was asleep, I wrote postcards to Mrs. Minato and the Matsumura family wishing them a happy, healthy New Year, and thanking them for their friendship. I also added the splendid news about Ko, and said, "I trust Ko will be able to walk in the near future. Her walking and Father's return are our strongest hopes and dreams."

As soon as I finished writing, I crawled under the bed and brought out the rice cakes and toothbrushes. I arranged them on each plate and left the tube of toothpaste in the center of the apple box. I covered it all with the evening newspaper.

"It's a beautiful New Year's Eve," Hideyo said as he came in. "I'll open the window a little more to let Ko see the stars. And you will be better able to hear the New Year's bell toll, Little One."

Ko woke. She told Hideyo that she'd been sitting up for five minutes. "The green tea did it!" he said, taking off his blanket. "Keep up that spirit!"

He sat down to relax and grabbed the newspaper to read. "What are these?" Hideyo cried excitedly. Ko's head turned to the table.

"Rice cakes and toothbrushes! New Year's presents for all of us!" I exclaimed. "Happy New Year to my Honorable Brother and Honorable Sister!"

"Oh, thank you, Little One! We really needed them!" Hideyo cried. He then put Ko's share of the celebration on her chest. I served Brother and Sister leftover tea.

"A toothbrush and a rice cake?" Ko was surprised, but her tone changed to scolding. "You are spending your earnings again, Little One! When are you going to learn to manage? You will never get yourself a new pair of shoes this way."

I echoed Hideyo. "New Year's comes but once a year and we live only once, so why not indulge ourselves with rice cakes and new toothbrushes!"

Hideyo burst out laughing.

As we sat sipping our tea and enjoying every bite of the sweet rice cakes, I told them what I had seen at the refugee center.

"We don't know how fortunate we are, until we see others in worse condition," said Hideyo. Ko and I both agreed strongly.

"Listen!" Hideyo said. "I hear the bells."

Hideyo leaned out the window and looked up into the sky. I sat straight up on the wooden floor in Japanese fashion, my knees folded with heels underneath my buttocks, tilting my good ear to hear the bells. None of us said a word. My mind reviewed our sad, hard, painful months. We did very well this year! I thought.

We were wrapped in stillness. Even the winter wind behaved. The bell would be tolling one hundred and eight times: one hundred times to get rid of all troubles and worries and to make good wishes for the next year, then eight more times to send the wishes to eight points of the compass. With each ring I wished in my heart, Father . . . come . . . home. The deep, serene sound of the bell mingled with my fragile dream, carrying the future's bright promise.

SILK THREAD

By the middle of January, Ko's sitting-up time had lengthened to ten minutes twice a day. Though she was right-handed, she trained herself to use her left. Hideyo made her a small, tray-like table from wood scraps he'd gathered near the burned-out warehouse where we used to live. Hideyo told Ko, "Now you can study, or do a little sewing."

Every time Ko heard that a patient was discharged from the hospital, she made me go to the hallway closet to see what had been discarded.

If the material was good enough to use, she would tear the garments apart while she was sitting up and then have me wash them. When the cloth was dry, I put it under Ko's futon to flatten, for we had no iron.

"You need a blouse and a skirt. You are growing, Little One!" Ko said. She then cut out the material for a blouse and told me to baste the pieces together with long, quick stitches. When that was done, she wanted me to try it on so that she could see to the fitting. Finally she told me to sew with fine stitches. I needed an iron to press the seams, so I peeled off the cover from a canteen and stuck it among the hot charcoals. When it was hot enough, I wrapped the canteen with my undershirt and pressed the seams with the round bottom. "Good idea!" Ko said. I felt I had accomplished a lot when I finished the blouse. I started on the skirt right away.

It was Ko's joy to see the silk fabrics Mrs. Suzuki had chosen for her son's name-day–blessing kimono. It was to be lined with white silk. "Feel this soft material, Little One!" said Ko.

"Lucky boy!" I said. Then I thought about all those beautiful silk kimonos we had had to leave in the bamboo grove. When we lived in Nanam, I took everything for granted and did not show any appreciation. Now, I had learned to appreciate every little thing that came my way.

Slowly, every day, Ko made progress on the kimono. But at the end of the day she was exhausted. Then she would fall fast asleep. When morning came, she wanted to start work right away while I did the morning chores. There were times when she was frustrated, for she could not use her left hand freely, and her right hand was useless. I offered to sew, but she was determined to do it herself. "You mind your silkworms and I'll mind my own work," said Ko.

All the silkworms had made cocoons, and I noticed that one of them had a tiny brownish hole on the tip. I took the cocoon to the window and used my broken magnifying lens to examine it carefully. The brownish hole was wet, and I saw a moth inside trying to widen the cocoon exit. I used Ko's sharply pointed scissors and cut a small round hole through another cocoon. I peeked inside. There was a brown pupa. This pupa was struggling, trying to peel off his skin to become a moth.

"What are you doing? You are late for school," Ko said.

"I am not going to school."

"Are you sick?"

"No. I want to watch my cocoons. It's Saturday. I will not miss much."

"No one is going to steal the cocoons. Go to school!"

"I want to see how the moths crawl out of their cocoons."

"Mother Nature teaches them how to do it. Don't worry about them. Just go to school! Now!" Ko commanded.

I knew what she was going to say next. "Honorable Brother is working hard to pay for your tuition. Do not waste his money. Right?"

"If you know so much, then just *go!*"

"This is an interesting project. I want to watch my cocoons closely. I have to make another journal . . . besides, I must exhibit the project at the city science fair."

"You do not know how lucky you are to have healthy legs to go to school." Ko was irritated. I caught on to her depression. It was Ko's dream as well as mine and Hideyo's for her to get out of bed and walk. Now she had important sewing to do, yet she could not even use her hands well. I knew better than to argue with her, so I dragged my rucksack out from beneath her bed. I left fried greens and cut-up dried seaweed on a plate for her snack. As I closed the door, I heard her voice behind my back: "Study well!"

Before the biology class began, Mr. Iwai asked if everyone was getting ready for the city science fair. If not, he'd have to fail students. He then praised my silkworm project. Sumiko gave me a nasty look. When Mr. Iwai came to my desk with several gadgets and a book about silk-worms, he said, "You will be needing these soon. Follow the book and study."

In the homeroom, Miss Asada gave us the new schedule of cleaning assignments. Sumiko said she did not want to be teamed with Kawashima Yoko. "But why?" asked the teacher.

Sumiko said, "She has been a troublemaker ever since she came to Sagano. There is no *peace* in the school anymore." Sumiko said that she wanted to make a motion for Kawashima Yoko to be suspended from school. I almost stood up to slap her mouth, but I held my temper by remembering: The more they pick on me, the more I must be serene.

With the gadgets and silkworm book in my ruck-sack, I trotted along to the hospital, wondering how many of the pupas had turned to moths and how many of them had crawled out. The more I thought about the cocoons, the faster I walked.

Suddenly something sharp, hard, and cold struck the back of my head. Shocked, I stag-gered. For a moment I blacked out. I sat on the ground until my vision cleared. I wanted to know what on earth had happened. Right next to my heels lay a huge, bloody tuna-fish head. Looking around to see where the fish head had flown from, I saw Sumiko darting inside her par-ents' fish market. Blood was streaming down my neck, and I was not sure whether it was the tuna's or mine. I picked up the fish head and ran to the hospital.

At the nurses' station, I asked one of the nurses to examine me. She immediately stuck my head over the stainless steel sink, ran water over my hair, and checked. "You are all right. There is no cut. Just a bump!" Another nurse asked, "What happened?"

I told them the tuna-fish head had flown down from the sky and hit me. I did not want Ko to know the truth.

"Luckily your skull is thick! Watch for flying objects next time," said the nurse who examined my head, laughing.

That night we ate one fourth of the tuna head. The rest I salted, wrapped in newspapers, tied securely, and hung on a nail outside of Ko's window.

Every evening after Hideyo left to check the buildings, Ko went to work on her project. I helped Ko hold the basted pieces tightly so that she could sew carefully with her left hand. When she needed to press a seam, I heated a canteen hot-water bottle. Ko would put a handkerchief over the bottle to protect the silk. But no matter how hard Ko tried, she could not sit up any longer than an hour at a time. "If I push myself to sew, the work will be a mess," she said.

I read the book *Silkworm*. Now I understood why Mr. Iwai had loaned me those gadgets.

They were thread pullers, spinners, and bobbins. The book told how to cook the cocoons and pull out the silk thread.

One morning I discovered that one of the moths in the box had laid her eggs and was dead. I saved the dead moth, for I wanted to exhibit it. When I told Mr. Iwai about the eggs, he said, "When the fair is over, I will take you to the silkworm farm, where they will keep the eggs until they hatch."

I began slowly cooking the cocoons in Mrs. Minato's cooking pot. While I went to school the cocoons stayed in the water. Then I cooked the cocoons again until loosened threads appeared. I pulled three threads from the cocoons and began spinning them to the spool.

Later Ko, smiling, told me her surgeon had seen the thread on the spinner and had said it was fine enough for surgical purposes! I decided to give the thread to Ko for her birthday.

I felt I had accomplished a lot when I learned the silkworm project was a success at the city science fair. I brought the silkworm eggs to the farm, and on my way home, I went to pick up some coal at the train-station switchyard. The sun had already set and it was getting dark.

"Young maiden! Young maiden!" someone

yelled. I stopped and looked around. "Yes, you! Are you a *deaf* young maiden?" It was Mr. Maki. He was pulling his wooden cart, huffing and puffing to catch up with me.

"Mr. Maki! Happy New Year! How have you been? How wonderful to run into you!" I showered my greetings upon him, for I had not seen him since the middle of November.

"Happy New Year? It's March. Time for plowing," said the old man. "You can help me soon, yes?"

"Of course I will. During the spring break," I answered. Mr. Maki told me his wife's arthritis had gotten worse and she could no longer help him in his field.

"By the way, what are you doing here at this time of day?" he asked.

"Picking coal at the switchyard." I pointed to my rucksack. "Coal lasts longer than wood." Then I asked him what he was doing so far away from his home. He said he was trying to make a living by selling rice and the vegetables that he'd stored in his root cellar during the winter.

"How is your sister?" he asked. As I helped pull his cart and we walked toward the hospital, I told him all our doings. At the crossroad, he said, "Here, I will give you a bag of rice in advance for your work, then I know you will show up!"

"I cannot pay back in work for that much rice," I cried. "I would have to work the rest of my life!"

"It's too heavy for an old man to bring all the way home," said Mr. Maki. He put the bag of rice on my shoulders with his shaking hands. "Hurry home, young maiden!" Pulling his wooden cart, he slowly made a left turn. Dark enveloped him completely, but the sound of his cart wheels rolling on the dirt road remained in my good ear for a long time.

Slowly the March sun melted the snow off the tip of Atago Mountain and the days lengthened. We began to hear nightingales early in the morning. Not only were the days longer, but Ko's sitting-up time was extended to an hour and a half twice a day. She finished making the little boy's name-day–blessing kimono. With the leftover white silk, Ko showed me how to make a white cap to go with the baby boy's special garment. I delivered them to Mrs. Suzuki. She was amazed at Ko's work. When I brought out the tiny white cap for her baby, she shed tears of joy.

Mrs. Suzuki spread word of Ko's sewing talent, and Ko began to receive notes from people requesting her to make some garments. This excited Ko. Whenever she sat up, she went to work, glad to earn some money for the household.

During the spring break I went to Mr. Maki's field and helped plow and sow seeds. Every time I went, Mrs. Maki gave me vegetables from her root cellar.

Each day, we checked our hospital mailbox to see if a return postcard had arrived from Father's birthplace. Hideyo wrote letters to the prime minister, but there was no response.

One day Hideyo came home earlier than Ko and I had expected him.

"Why so early?" Ko asked worried. "Are you ill?"

Hideyo said he had not wanted to tell us until he was sure, but two weeks ago, while digging ditches in front of a construction office he had seen an ad in the window: WANTED! SKILLFUL, HEALTHY YOUNG MEN. So during the lunch hour, while everyone else was eating, Hideyo went to the construction office and applied. They gave him tests in reading, arithmetic, geometry, writing, and appreciation of the arts, as well as psychological tests. The next day at lunchtime he had to go for a physical checkup. They told him to come back today. He was hired!

"Now, I can sleep an hour and a half longer," Hideyo said, smiling, "I really need it."

"What will you be doing for the construction company?" asked Ko. "Is it very dangerous work?"

"No more dangerous than digging ditches with a pick," he said. His new work would be following blueprints to build government offices and temporary shelters for refugees. And, because the job was based in Maizuru, Hideyo would be able take Father's name posters to paste on the refugee-center wall.

"I never did like to let Little One go there alone," he said. "The wonderful thing is, I have Sundays off from the construction company. But I still want to keep up the security work until the hospital bill is paid."

Hideyo liked his new job. Whenever the company discarded boards, he brought them home. He gathered nails that were dropped on the ground. "We have to build our own shed. Someday Ko will be released from here," Hideyo said, laying the boards neatly on the floor. "Put my bedding over them."

He borrowed a hammer and a saw from the construction site and built Ko a lawn chair with a straight back and rollers for the legs. Whenever it was warm on Sundays, Hideyo and I would pick Ko up and put her in the chair. He would take Ko out to the hospital grounds for as long as she was able to sit up. He even made Ko fabric holders that attached to her work tray with two wooden pieces and a spring.

Every day Ko went to work for her new customers. The problem was that she did not have an iron, so she had to wait for me to come home to help with the canteens. But soon the problem was settled. While building a government office, Hideyo noticed that the small angle irons used to secure the T-shaped posts were the wrong size. He told the foreman about the danger and asked to change them. When it was done, Hideyo saved all the discarded angle irons. He split one in two and attached a wooden stick as a handle to make Ko a flat, square iron! He made two of them so that Ko could stick one in the low-burning charcoal to heat while she was using the other one.

Ko's hospital room was filling up with discarded construction materials. Hideyo's futon bed was almost as high as Ko's bed because he kept on stacking wooden boards beneath it. Hideyo told me to move out from under Ko's bed and sleep by the door so that he could store more material. We left Ko's chair in the corridor.

When the double cherry flowers painted the late-spring sky pink, the surgeon removed the plaster casts from Ko's legs and right arm and immediately put on braces. "You may try to stand for a few moments," he said. Hideyo presented Ko with a pair of crutches he had made. The doctor, nurses, Hideyo, and I made a circle around Ko. Hideyo's worried eyes were fixed on our sister. Ko was very shaky and was biting her lips as if to say she was determined to stand. The doctor said that if she felt comfortable standing, she might take a step.

She leaned on the crutches to take a step, but her right arm was so weak that her body tilted to the left. Awkwardly, fearfully, she moved her right leg forward.

"Excellent! Keep on trying," Hideyo encouraged Ko. But Ko could take no more steps. Suddenly she became white as a sheet and fainted. Everybody jumped to keep Ko from falling to the floor.

From then on, every day, Ko woke me early in the morning for standing practice, and every evening when Hideyo got home for his thirty-minute break from his security rounds, Ko insisted that I stand a few steps ahead of her and that Hideyo stand behind. She would push the crutches forward and slowly drag her legs to come even with the crutches.

"Keep on! Take another step! That's it! One more step!" cheered Hideyo. "Remember, you were born in the Year of the Horse—trot like a horse!"

Though Ko learned to take several steps comfortably, Hideyo gave Ko strict orders never to practice walking alone.

Ko was more motivated day by day. Her right fingers were still swollen, but the surgeon gave her hand and finger exercises, and told her to take everything slowly.

Once she learned how to slip off her bed, she leaned on her crutches and began to do the easy tasks of boiling water and sponge bathing. If she ran into difficulties, she invented ways to accomplish what she wanted. During the day, for about an hour, a nurse would take the braces from Ko's legs and give her exercises. Ko sighed painfully and gritted her teeth. Whenever she had to bend her knees as far as she could, tears rolled down her cheeks. Finally the day came when Ko was able to walk without braces, though she still needed crutches.

Because Ko was now able to do light chores in her room, instead of going home as fast as I could after school, I often went to Mr. Maki's field to weed. Or I would go straight to the train switchyard to pick up coal. If I had time, I would go to sell my own wares from door to door. Ko was busy making customers' garments, so I made aprons, baby kimonos, bibs, and beanbag toys.

Whenever we three had our supper, the subject of discussion was where we could live after Ko was released from the hospital. I said I could live anywhere as long as it was not the train station. Hideyo thought it would be best to build a shack near the hospital so that he could keep his evening job.

Although he did not have to work, Hideyo got up as early as usual on Sundays. After taking Ko for a walk around the corridor, he would put her in the lawn chair he had made and take her outside. While they read books together, I did the chores. Then, when Ko was napping, Hideyo would go to look for places where he could build us a shack. I would go sell my wares. Every time I came home with earnings, Ko would put them away in a secret pocket in the wrapping cloth, saying, "It is going to stay there until you have enough for a new pair of shoes."

One Sunday, in the late afternoon, Hideyo came home from his search with a decision. "I will build under the concrete bridge on the upper stream of the Kamigamo River." Hideyo told us there were lots of homeless people living there, some in their own shacks, and some without even a roof over their heads. Until he could pay off the hospital bill, we would have to live that way. Then we would look for a rooming house.

SHACK UNDER THE BRIDGE

When the cuckoo birds' love song echoed in early June, Ko was released from the hospital. The moving day was Sunday. Hideyo and I put as many boards as we could across our backs and walked the three miles to our spot under the bridge. The long, narrow boards stuck far out like pairs of wings, and the passersby went around us to avoid getting hurt.

The bridge support was a solid concrete wall. Hideyo planned to make a lean-to shack against this wall. I guarded our things so that he could make more trips to the hospital for wider boards. While he was building, I took the streetcar to Mr. Maki's and borrowed his wooden cart.

I piled Ko, her futon, and the wrapping-cloth bundle onto the cart and pulled the cart to the bridge. Pulling that weight wore me out. From the edge of the bank, I called Hideyo to help, for I could not roll the cart down the steep slope.

Hideyo left Ko and me on the street. He held tightly to the cart handle, slowly letting the wheels roll down the slope to the shack. Then Hideyo carried Ko to our new home on his back. I unloaded our belongings right away.

Now Ko stayed and guarded our things. Hideyo and I pulled the cart up to the bridge and went to the hospital. He loaded on as much as he could and took off for the bridge. I stayed behind to pack the rest of our things in the portable cabinet Mrs. Minato had left us and in the apple box.

Hideyo made one more trip with the cart. When the room was empty, I cleaned it as best I could, for it had been our home for the past nine months. I checked the hallway closet and took the discarded bedclothes. I said farewell and thanks to the nurses. They said everyone was going to miss us. One nurse said, "If Ko needs help, do not hesitate to come."

Hideyo was quick about building a shack. When I returned, he had a board floor in place. Ko looked tired, and I quickly made a bed for her.

Ko said if I fetched water and built a fire, she'd try to cook something while I returned the cart. "It will be stolen if we leave it here overnight. Go now and hurry back," Ko said. "We have to straighten things up before dark."

The homeless men and women, young adults and small ones, gathered around our shack and watched as Hideyo continued his carpentry. Their undernourished bodies were covered by filthy rags. Hideyo introduced himself to them in a loud voice and added, "These are my little sisters, Ko and Yoko." We bowed slightly. Instead of greetings, they just stared at us as if we were their foes. I tried to smile at them, but I could not. I was scared that they might harm us.

A boy, about seventeen, fixed his eyes on the scraps of wood around the shack. His keloid-scarred face, neck, and hands were painful to look at.

"Do you want these to build a fire?" I fearfully asked, thinking his mother could use them. Without a word he made a pocket with his shirt. His stomach was severely burned and his flesh was infected. I gave him the wood scraps.

He left us for a while then returned. "Sister, can I have some more?" This time Hideyo picked up more scraps and gave them to him. The boy returned again and again. Hideyo told the boy he had taken enough scraps to build a fire and that we had to keep some for ourselves. But the boy said, "They are not enough to cremate my father who has been dead the past two days."

"What?" Hideyo shouted. "Show me where your father is!"

I tried to follow my brother. "Do not go, Little One!" said Ko firmly.

Soon Hideyo and the boy returned. Hideyo gave us a sad nod and put his arms around the boy.

The boy, Yasuo, said they were *Hibakusha*, meaning atom-bomb victims. His mother and baby sister died in Nagasaki. He and his father had come to their relatives in Kyoto, but they were refused help.

Hideyo had to go back to work at the hospital, but told Yasuo he would call the police. He had read in the newspaper about special privileges for atom-bomb victims. Within a couple of hours, I saw a group of policemen with bright flashlights. They carted Yasuo's father away. Yasuo followed the cart, crying loudly, "Daddy, I want to die, too! I want to go with you where Mother and Ettchan live!"

The shack Hideyo built was about the same size as Ko's hospital room. We had no electricity. Until Hideyo came home, Ko sat in her lawn chair, wrapped in a blanket. She kept a shichirin fire burning low and the teakettle hot.

I eased my way into the dark shack to pile the wrapping-cloth bundle and our belongings in a corner against the bridge's concrete wall. I made our futon beds. On the other side of the river, houses with twinkling lights in their windows made me envious. I now regretted that I had complained about the dim lights of the four-tatami-mat room in the warehouse and the hospital room. Ko told me to go to bed, as tomorrow was a school day. But in my mind, I saw the homeless people's despairing eyes floating here and there in the dark. I could not go to sleep. I wished Hideyo would come home.

"No moon even, to give us a light," I grumbled. Ko said if I went to sleep, the morning would come quickly. I said, "I am scared to go to sleep for fear someone will take our things.

"Let's sing!" I suggested. "It has been a long time since we sang a duet together."

"Let's try Father's favorite, 'The Birthplace!'" said Ko. So we began in low voices:

"The mountain where we chased rabbits
The river where we fished little carp
Nostalgia still thrives in my heart
Unable to forget my birthplace!"

Just as we finished the first verse, a whistled tune came nearer and nearer. I knew it was Hideyo. He always used to join us by whistling when we sang. As he sat in front of the shichirin, he whistled the song from the beginning. Ko and I listened. His beautiful whistling joined the soft murmur of the river and carried into the midnight air. I wished Father could hear the tune and sense our earnest desire to have him with us.

I was wakened by a strong thud and rain splashing on the siding. I worried if Ko was warm and dry in the wind and rain. In the dark I looked for my blanket.

"*No!*" yelled Hideyo, who was sleeping by the entrance, which had no door. I heard him get up and go around the shed.

"Say! Whoever you are," he yelled, "this is our house! Not a public toilet! Do it somewhere else!"

I could not sleep after that. As soon as the eastern sky turned to pale pink, I filled buckets of water and washed the siding clean.

Hideyo handed Ko a couple of books he had borrowed from the university library. "Fine books," he said. I was so sleepy that I did not want to go to school. But I left Ko a rice ball and small pieces of dried seaweed and water in a canteen to drink, and then I went.

I could not concentrate on my schoolwork, thinking about Ko alone in our shack. What if someone harmed her? How would she defend herself? I should have told her, before I left, that she should keep her peeling knife nearby for protection. I could not help but imagine the bad things that could be happening to Ko. I could not wait for school to end so that I could get back to her.

When I saw Mr. Naido in the furnace room, I told him about our new home. He was glad that Ko was out of the hospital but terribly sorry that we had to live under the bridge. "Just for a while, until Brother pays up the hospital bills," I said cheerfully. "But I do miss the electricity. We have to do everything in the daylight." I asked him if there was any discarded india ink. He had several small bottles that the students had thrown away. I poured all the ink into a larger jar.

As soon as school was over, I flew down the stony bank to our shack. Ko was sitting in her chair by the entrance, guarding our house and reading a book, but she looked sick.

"Have you eaten?" I asked.

She shook her head and said she wanted to take a nap, as she had not slept at all the night before. She scooted herself off her chair and went to her bed. She was wearing her braces on her legs and the sling on her right arm. She must be in pain, I thought. I remembered the surgeon had said that whenever she felt pain, she must wear the braces. I felt Ko's toes. They were icy cold. I quickly built a fire and boiled water in a bucket. I filled the canteens, and also the hot-water bottle, which was still borrowed from Dr. Yamada. I put them all around Ko. I covered her up with Hideyo's and my blankets.

"Thank you. I was cold," said Ko. Soon she fell off to sleep.

While our supper was cooking over a low fire, I wrote on the siding with a fat brush dipped in india ink, KAWASHIMA RESIDENCE. DO NOT GO TO THE TOILET!

Hideyo came home, carrying a few discarded

long boards and nails. He made a door that had a square window, but no glass. Even though Hideyo was pounding and making noise attaching the door to the shack, Ko did not wake up.

It was terribly noisy. Whenever traffic went over the bridge our shack shook, and it was worse when the heavy American army trucks roared above us. The shack shook like leaves in a strong wind, and dirt poured over the roof like bullets. On the third night under the bridge we mistook an army convoy for an earthquake—Hideyo dragged Ko out of the shack to the river flats.

Night after night Ko stayed awake, saying she could not sleep for fear someone might burst into our home to harm us or steal the material that belonged to her customers. So it was Ko who played clock and woke me up early each morning to prepare for school.

While I was at school, if it was a clear day Ko would open the shack door and sit in her chair to do her sewing. She hated days when it rained. It was dark in the shack and she could not see well enough to make fine stitches. Rain made her entire body ache. Then she worried that the rain would ruin the customers' material. She would wrap the material in a blanket and cover it with thick, hardened, oiled newspapers to keep the cloth dry. The oiled papers were scraps that Hideyo had picked up from the construction site.

When I returned from school, Ko scooted off her chair and moved quickly to her futon. As soon as she lay down on her bed, she fell fast asleep until midnight.

I asked Ko one day, "What do you do during the night when Hideyo and I are asleep?" Because there was no electricity, she could not even read a book.

She said, "It is a fine time to meditate and plan in my head how I can help Hideyo get us out from under this bridge."

By now it was mid-July. A month had passed since we'd moved into the shack. When the sun hit the bridge during the day, it became extremely hot. We could stand the heat, but when the humidity rose, the shack turned into a steam bath.

At night mosquitoes arrogantly attacked and sucked our blood. I was covered with mosquito bites. I was constantly scratching here and there, and often the bumps bled. While Ko was sleeping late one afternoon, I stealthily took my money from the secret pocket of the wrapping-cloth bundle and ran to a nearby general store for mosquito coils. When night came I lit them.

"You got into the wrapping-cloth pocket!" said Ko.

"I did."

When Ko found out the price of the coils, she took her own money from the cloth pouch that she kept with her at all times. Ko put her money into the wrapping-cloth pocket. "Don't touch your earnings!" said Ko. "They are for your shoes."

Hideyo did not permit Ko to walk alone even when she wore her braces and used the crutches. He said, "Unlike the hospital corridor, the river field is rough, and she might slip and fall on the rocks." However, I noticed that Ko had lost interest in walking. I thought it was from not having enough sleep and from the heat. But whenever she sat in her chair she would gently rub her legs, and she ate less and less. Her feet were always cold during the night, so I filled the canteen hot-water bottles for her before I went to sleep. Hideyo said that in a couple of months the hospital bill would be paid, and then we could move into a rooming house. "Persevere, Sisters!" he said.

Before summer vacation at the end of July, Mr. Iwai asked if I would be interested in working as a helper in the research department of a silk textile company. He said he also worked there during the summer. I took the job.

I liked working at the research department. It was a happy day when I came home with my first pay, in cash, in the company's envelope. Ko took it away from me and hid it in the wrapping-cloth pocket. She said she would guard it so that I could not sneak into it.

Every morning Ko sat up and leaned on the concrete wall and woke me by calling "Little One." But one morning she did not. I was wakened instead by Ko's moaning. I knew right away that something was terribly wrong. Ko was still in her bed. I put my hand on her forehead. She was burning. "What's wrong?" I asked. She said her right leg was in great pain and she asked if I would go to the hospital to get medicine before I went to the research department.

"Why didn't you tell me sooner that you were in pain?" I asked, feeling very frustrated.

"I did not want to worry you or Brother," she said, wiping her tears.

I ran to the river to fetch cold water. I soaked a thin washcloth, wrung it out, and put it on Ko's forehead. Quickly I washed myself and gave her water from a canteen to drink. It had been boiled the night before, so I knew it was safe. Then I ran all the way to the hospital.

I burst into the nurses' station. A familiar nurse was there, turning the pages of patients' records. I was gasping and tried to say why I had come, but I was panting so hard that the nurse could not understand what I was saying.

"It is about your sister, isn't it?" she asked. I nodded. She gave me a glass of water to drink and a piece of gauze to wipe my sweaty face. I asked for medicine. The nurse took notes and asked me questions, but I could not answer them all. Ko had only just told me about the pains. The nurse said it would be best to bring Ko to the hospital quickly. "In the meantime," she said, unlocking the medicine cabinet and handing me a small bottle of medicine, "give this to your sister.

The dosage is printed on the bottle. I will report Ko's condition to her doctor."

I headed out of the hospital. In my haste I almost bumped into a woman. "Miss Yoko!" she cried. It was Mrs. Minato. She looked well in a pretty summer kimono. We exchanged greetings with deep bows. She said she had come to the hospital for her checkup. She had left her home early so that she could visit with us. I told her we now lived under the bridge and that Ko was very ill. "I must get back to her right away."

When I said "under the bridge" and "Ko is ill," Mrs. Minato's expression changed. She looked at her watch and firmly said, "Wait for me in the waiting room!"

Because my mind was fixed on Ko and wanting to bring the medicine to her, the time I spent waiting for Mrs. Minato moved slowly. I wished I had not met her at the entrance. I said to myself, I could be at our shack by now!

I went to the nurses' station to borrow the telephone. I called the research department and left a message that my sister was very ill and I could not come to work. When I returned to the waiting room Mrs. Minato came in. "When things are settled, I will come see you," I said. "I have no time now."

"We will talk while we walk to the bridge."

"You mean, you are going to visit my sister?" I asked. She nodded. Because Mrs. Minato was wearing a summer kimono and clogs, she could only take small steps. I had no choice but to walk slowly and listen to what she had to say.

She said she had not forgotten us, but her mother had died from a massive stroke two months earlier. She was sad, and had been busy straightening out her mother's belongings. "But the happy news is that my husband finally returned safely from abroad and has started an express delivery agency. The business is small, but we are managing. I have been telling him about you and your brother and sister. Now tell me all about yourselves."

In the warmth of such a gracious woman, I suddenly released my tension. All I could do was sob.

"Where is the bridge?" Mrs. Minato asked.

I pointed and tried to tell her what we had been doing, but I could not utter a word. I kept on crying. She took hold of my hand as we walked.

Ko was surprised to see our unexpected guest. She tried to get up to greet Mrs. Minato, but she could not. Mrs. Minato took the washcloth from Ko's forehead. "Hot!" she yelled. I soaked a towel again and put it on Ko's forehead. Ko took her medicine.

"Let's get you to the hospital!" said Mrs. Minato.

"I will be all right," Ko said.

Mrs. Minato scurried up the hill and stopped a taxi. "Let's go!" she yelled.

"I cannot burden Brother any more with bills," said Ko firmly.

"Do not argue now!" said Mrs. Minato.

"You must go," I urged Ko, "just to find out what is wrong with your leg. You may be able to come home right away!" I handed her the crutches. She would not move. I said, "Honorable Sister, the taxi is waiting. It's costing us. You always told me never to waste money!"

Ko was hesitating. But finally she said, "Just for a checkup." When she got up, she staggered. I grabbed her from the back. Mrs. Minato and I helped Ko up the hill and the taxi driver came to help Ko into the taxi. Mrs. Minato sat next to the driver. Before the taxi drove off, Ko said, "For supper, cook together last night's leftovers."

"I understand!" I hollered over the taxi's loud motor. I could see Mrs. Minato urging the driver to hurry.

All alone at the riverbank, I longed for Father. He always had a peaceful solution for our troubles. After solving a problem, he made his family feel at ease. He'd smilingly ask, "Now, was that a big problem?" I felt like screaming, Father, we *do* have problems! Only you can settle matters by coming back to us!

The sun was getting high. I figured it was about ten or eleven o'clock. I made Ko's bed so that she could go right to sleep as soon as she returned. I untied the wrapping-cloth bundle to straighten out what was inside. Mother's ashes in the mess kit and our family treasure, the ancestors' sword, were carefully wrapped. I put those aside with deep respect. Then I dumped out everything else. At the bottom there was a newspaper. I picked it up to read. There was Ko's huge brush writing in india ink: KEEP YOUR MITTS OFF! IT IS FOR YOUR SHOES! BOSSY SISTER!

I burst out laughing, but at the same time a great sense of loneliness attacked me from every angle. I swallowed lumps in my throat and tried hard not to cry. I put everything back into the wrapping cloth neatly, except our socks. "Until Hideyo gets home, I will mend them," I decided. I brought them outside the shack. Leaning against the shack wall, I put my hand into each sock to check for holes, but Ko had already mended them all. She must have done it while I was in school. Sew some beanbags instead, I said to myself. Using Ko's sewing tray, I began to cut up scraps of material.

"Miss Yoko!" someone called from afar. It was Mrs. Minato.

I ran to her. "What happened to my sister?" I asked.

She said the nurses had wheeled Ko to the X-ray room. "They do not know what is wrong," she said. "Your sister must stay in the hospital until the fever is gone." I felt like spanking myself for not keeping my eyes on Ko's legs more closely.

Mrs. Minato examined our shack. She said it was well-built from scrap materials, but we could not stay in it.

"My mother's room is unused. It is an eight-tatami-mat room. I shall rent it to you."

"We have no money to pay the rent. Thank you anyway," I said.

"You can help me with errands, and your brother can help repair our house. My husband is no carpenter," said Mrs. Minato. "I am going home now, but I will be back as soon as possible."

I asked her the time. "Almost three," she said. She went to the street and waited for a taxi.

Two and a half more hours until Hideyo comes, I thought. I made two beanbags. Then I built the fire, filled the teakettle full of hot water, and slowly cooked the leftovers, the way Ko wanted.

Mrs. Minato returned with her husband. He drove a small Datsun truck and parked it by the edge of the bank. Mr. Minato was just as short as his wife, with thick eyebrows and a tanned pleasant face. We exchanged our greetings. He smiled, bowed, and thanked me for looking after his wife while she was in the hospital.

"Let us have some tea, and tell us what you have been doing," said Mrs. Minato. She brought a package of green tea from her kimono sleeve. I told her about how Ko made a man-child's name-day–blessing kimono and about my silkworm project. "Also, I am getting better at stitching," I said.

Hideyo came home. He was very surprised to see Mr. and Mrs. Minato. When I broke the news to him about Ko, Hideyo thanked our friends for taking our sister to the hospital. Mr. Minato wasted no time and urged us to move into their house. Hideyo gratefully accepted their offer but he said he wanted to stay with Ko in the hospital, and go to work from there. "Your little sister will be safe while you are with Miss Ko," the Minatos assured him.

Mr. Minato packed Ko's and Hideyo's bedding into his truck. I shoved Ko's nightclothes, Hideyo's underwear, and their toilet articles into Ko's rucksack. Hideyo ate his supper quickly. I packed what was left in Ko's mess kit and gave it to Hideyo so that she would have something to eat.

"Prepare to move while I take your brother to the hospital," said Mr. Minato.

"Little One, I will come back to you as soon as I can," said Hideyo. He bowed deeply in appreciation to Mr. and Mrs. Minato.

Mr. Minato neatly piled all our belongings into the truck. Before I left our shack, I smeared india ink over the Kawashima name on the siding, then wrote in huge letters, VACANT HOUSE! I rode in the back of the truck with our belongings, holding tightly to the wrapping-cloth bundle to make sure it would not bounce out onto the road when Mr. Minato went over potholes. The sun was about to set, and I hoped someone would go into the shack for a good night's sleep. I felt I was richly blessed to be moving into a real house.

WITH THE MINATOS

Mr. and Mrs. Minato had an old, small house by Hiei Mountain. They led me to the eight-tatami-mat room, which was separated from their living quarters. I was excited to see a low study desk with a reading lamp, and a small wall clock, with its pendulum swaying. I turned on the ceiling light by pulling down on a string. The entire room brightened. How good to have electricity once again! In addition to all this, there was a closet big enough to hold our futons and belongings.

Mr. Minato and I unloaded everything. For the time being, I put it all in a corner of the room. Mrs. Minato showed me the water pump and the toilet. She then took me to a small kitchen where her mother used to cook. There were two shichirin, and some charcoal in a box nearby. "You are welcome to use these," she said, and added, "Let me know of whatever else you need." She then went to fix the three of us something to eat, saying, "It's our reunion day!"

Moving into my friend's house made me feel relaxed and happy. I piled my schoolbooks on the corner of the broad desktop. I put away some papers I'd picked up from the furnace room in a deep side drawer. In a smaller drawer I stored pencil stubs, a ruler, erasers, and a compass. I saved the rest of the empty drawers for

Ko. Then I turned on the reading lamp and wrote to Corporal Matsumura. After asking how he and his wife were doing, I told him our news and gave him our new address. Suddenly I felt exhausted. I pulled my futon near the desk and the lamp so that I could lie down. The eight-tatami-mat room seemed enormous compared to the other places where we had lived since leaving the bamboo grove.

Later I went to the pump to wash and tidy myself for Mrs. Minato's supper table. My stomach was growling, for I had eaten nothing all day, except a rice bowl full of green tea with Mr. and Mrs. Minato by the shack.

I thought I would devour Mrs. Minato's delicacies, but thinking of Ko's suffering churned my stomach. "You need to eat," said Mr. Minato putting a few more sashimi on my small plate. I asked him if I might save my portion for Ko's lunch the next day. I thought Ko's fever would blow away if she could taste the good fish. Mr. Minato said the sashimi would not stay fresh, so I must eat it all up. Mrs. Minato said that she had saved a fish for Hideyo and Ko, and I could cook it for them after supper. "So enjoy yours!" she said.

The next morning, I was wakened by a rooster crowing. They have chickens, I thought. I have not eaten a whole egg for almost three and a half years! I want to make scrambled eggs and take them to Ko for her breakfast. Sister will be surprised, and heal in no time! The wall clock said five-fifty-five. Though it was early, I pumped water to wash my face. I felt rested: It was the first time since we left Nanam that I had slept soundly, as a human being should.

I looked at the surroundings in the morning light. There were miniature bamboo shrubs all around the Minatos' house, and our eight-tatami-mat room faced a tiny flower garden with a narrow wooden porch. Beyond stood Hiei Mountain. When I heard the rooster crow again, I looked around to see the henhouse. But there was none. Then I saw, over the bamboo hedge, hog- and henhouses that belonged to the house next door.

I introduced myself to the neighbor and asked if she would sell me two eggs. The neighbor, Mrs. Kinoshita, was busy cooking breakfast. She did not stop what she was doing, but said, "Pick your own eggs. Leave the money in the box. Three eggs for five yen."

Instead of two, I scrambled three eggs. I was tempted to eat a bit of them, but I thought it would be much nicer if I ate with Ko. I packed our breakfast in my mess kit along with the fish I'd cooked after supper. I filled my canteen with clear water. Before I left my new home, I made sure the charcoal fire was out. I asked Mrs. Minato if there was a streetcar to the hospital.

"There is a bus every hour that takes you right here," she said.

"If my sister is feeling better, I will go to the research department. Otherwise I will be at the hospital." Mrs. Minato handed me two apples to take to Ko.

Ko's room was five doors down from where she'd stayed before. She was asleep. I went to the nurses' station to let them know I was there. The familiar nurse who'd given me the bottle of medicine handed me a note from Hideyo.

LITTLE ONE, THE SURGEON SAID KO'S RIGHT KNEE IS BADLY INFECTED AND HE IS GOING TO OPERATE ON HER THIS AFTERNOON. IF THIS IS NOT SUCCESSFUL, THEN THEY ARE GOING TO AMPUTATE HER LEG. I BEGGED THE SURGEON NOT TO LET KO KNOW ABOUT HER CONDITION. SO BE CHEERFUL AROUND HER. DO STAY WITH HER TODAY. I WILL BE HOME AS FAST AS I CAN. THANKS FOR YOUR HELP.

My tears fell on the paper. Ko must have suffered a long time with this, just because she did not want to burden Hideyo with more bills! Wiping my eyes, I said to the nurse, "I have brought my sister scrambled eggs for breakfast."

"The surgery is scheduled for 1 P.M. Miss Ko should not eat now," said the nurse. "We have given your sister a shot to relax her, so you should not wake her." I let the research department know that I would be absent again. Then I did my hospital chores.

Ko woke up. She said she had heard that we'd moved to Mrs. Minato's, but why wasn't I at work? I told her I missed her so much that I just had to come see her. She said it was about time that I grew up. "What will you do if I die?" she asked. I told her she was too tough to die. But deep inside I trembled, knowing that she might lose her right leg very soon.

"I do not feel any pain now," said Ko. "The doctor will let me go home this evening as soon as Brother gets back. So go on, go to work."

"I already called the company."

"Little One!" she said firmly. "Get to work! I'll see you this evening."

"You will like our eight-tatami-mat room." I forced myself to smile. "It is in a quiet rural area with a flower garden and miniature bamboo shrubs. This morning a neighbor's rooster gave me a wake-up call."

"That sounds good. Now get to work."

"I do not want to go to work."

"Whether you want to or not, if a job is offered to you, you must take it with appreciation. Be faithful!"

"I understand and I will go!" I did not want to frustrate her before the operation. "Is there anything more I can do?"

"I can take care of myself!" my sister said.

I showed Ko the mess kit, which held the scrambled eggs and cooked flounder. I flashed apples and chopsticks. "These are for our supper," I said, leaving them all in the corner. I decided I would go to the train-station switch-yard to pick up some coal.

Before I left, I checked the hospital mailbox. Because Hideyo still worked there, he'd kept Ko's mailbox and changed the name to Kawashima Hideyo. It was empty. I wondered if we would ever hear from Father. If the Russian government told us that Father was dead, then we would accept our fate. Not knowing if he was dead or alive really frustrated me. If Father was alive somewhere, then he *must* come home to us. No one could measure our love and respect for Father.

I gathered coal until my rucksack was filled. Ko is in the operating room by now, I thought, hastening my steps toward the hospital.

In front of her parents' fish market, I met Sumiko, who had just returned from playing tennis. Waving her racket to show that she was one of the trendy rich girls, she said she hadn't seen me lately. I told her that we had moved to the Tanaka area. "What?" she shouted. "Tanaka? *Burakumin* live there!" Burakumins are social outcasts.

"So?" I said. "They are very *good* people." I stressed the word good.

"Maybe you are a Burakumin and have been

hiding your identity all this time!" She spat near me and spitefully said, "Do me a favor. Stay away from our fish market."

I felt like pulling her hair by the roots and sticking her head into a tub full of smelly fish innards for discriminating against the Burakumin. Stay serene, I said to myself, and ran all the way to Ko's room.

Ko was still in surgery. I sat on the floor and thought about the Burakumin. Some called them four-legged animals or dirty people. Their history began way back in the twelfth century in the Heian period. They were excluded from regular village communities. They were made to handle dead animals and dead people.

Now, in the twentieth century, Burakumin jobs include grave digging, butchering, tanning, and creating leather footwear and jackets. The Burakumin were able to live in towns, but they were still segregated. Some lived in shacks still, but some had built themselves houses. No matter how bright they were, they were never able to go to prestigious schools or get the jobs they might have wanted. They could not marry non-Burakumin. It is discrimination, I fumed. There's nothing wrong with being Burakumin. They have carried their burden from generation to generation. Mr. and Mrs. Minato live strongly, and to me they have a beautiful existence.

Hideyo and the surgeon came to the room while I was thinking. The surgeon said he and his team had first thought they must amputate Ko's leg, but they'd saved it. "I want to warn you," said the surgeon. "Miss Ko's right leg will never bend again. You must inform her about it. If you cannot, I will."

"She can walk, can't she?" Hideyo and I both asked the same question at once.

"Of course, she can. I will check on her later."

Knowing Hideyo had to leave on his first round, I gave him the scrambled eggs, cooked fish, and water to drink. "Eggs and fish!" Hideyo was excited, and asked me how I felt about sleeping alone in an unfamiliar place.

"Very peaceful! You and Ko will like the surroundings!" Hideyo nodded, satisfied by my words. His actions, the way he spoke, and even the way he nodded resembled Father more and more these days.

"I am thankful!" Hideyo said. "I cannot imagine how Ko would feel if she woke up and found out her leg was gone. I am grateful they saved her leg! I am also grateful that you met Mrs. Minato!"

"Me, too!"

The nurses wheeled Ko in. She was unconscious. Unexpectedly, Mr. Minato came in with them. "I happened to be delivering some furniture nearby," he said. "My wife wanted me to check on you and Miss Ko."

I told Mr. Minato that I wanted to stay at the hospital until Ko was released. He said he would bring my futon and some cooking and eating utensils as soon as he could. I did not know what to do about the wrapping-cloth bundle, which held the sword, Mother's ashes, and my earnings. But I felt it would be safe to leave in the eight-tatami-mat room.

When Hideyo came back for his thirty-minute break, he was smiling. I had never seen him look so happy. I thought it was probably because the surgeon had saved Ko's leg.

"Little One! Look at this!" he said, showing me a long white official envelope. Special delivery from Father's birthplace! I was excited. Hideyo opened it and pulled out a worn, narrow, brownish envelope.

"What is it? Hurry up!" I demanded. The envelope was addressed to Mother in Father's handwriting! It was all the way from Russia!

"From Father!" I exclaimed, and I could not close my mouth for a couple of seconds. "Father is alive! He is alive!" I screamed. Then I choked up and cried. "What did Father say?" I asked.

Hideyo showed me a piece of paper that was censored and smeared with black ink. We couldn't see the writing.

"What is this?" I shouted. "These Communists!"

But Hideyo pointed to the edge of the paper, saying, "Read this."

I brought the paper beneath the dim light to see things clearly. Father had written in pencil, at the end, very faintly, "I shall be home before long."

"He is coming home! He is coming home!" I wiped away my tears, and jumped up and down at the same time. In the excitement, Ko woke up. "Honorable Sister, Father is alive! He is coming home!" I cried. Hideyo hushed me so that I would not disturb neighboring patients.

Ko was still groggy and asked, "What's going on? What's wrong with my leg?"

"Father is alive! He is coming home!" I shouted. I could not control the joy. I wanted to let the whole world know that Father was coming home.

Hideyo explained to Ko that the doctors had operated on her badly infected right knee. "They have saved the leg instead of amputating it. However, it will never bend again. Do you understand me clearly? Your leg is saved, but it will not bend anymore."

Ko was quiet. She bit her lips and said mildly, "You mean I cannot fold my knees to sit upon a tatami floor anymore?"

"No. But there will be chairs for all of us to sit upon!" Hideyo smiled. "We will adopt the Western style of living!"

"The splendid news is that Father is alive, and coming home!" I said, romping about.

"Honest? You are not lying to make me feel better?" Ko asked. Hideyo showed her Father's censored letter and pointed at the edge of the paper. She focused her eyes on the faint print.

"Ahhhhhhh!" Ko cried.

Mr. and Mrs. Minato brought my futon and, in the apple-box table and portable cabinet, the things we really needed to stay at the hospital. Hideyo showed them the letter from Father. They kept on shouting, "Congratulations!"

Before I crawled under Ko's bed to sleep, I wrote to tell Corporal Matsumura the splendid news that Father was coming home.

If the doctor had allowed Ko, she would have left the hospital the next day to prepare for Father's homecoming. Very often before I left for work, she made me go to the hallway closet to see if any men's bedclothes had been discarded. She wanted to make kimonos for Father.

Hideyo notified Father's birthplace of our new address and kept on sending the town hall return postcards, requesting to be told as soon as Father appeared to register his name.

Though Ko's temperature ran high, she often lied and said she felt good and was ready to go home. Finally, a month after the operation, she was released. Mr. Minato came with his truck on Sunday and moved us.

Both Hideyo and Ko liked our new home. However, Ko and I did not see Hideyo until after midnight during the week, because Hideyo went straight from the construction site to the hospital. He spent his thirty-minute break in the waiting room reading books.

Early every Sunday morning when the weather was good, Hideyo, Ko, and I went for a walk. Because I was wearing Ko's shoes, she wore straw slippers made for her by Mr. Minato. Ko was still using crutches, tilting her body to the left so that she would not put much weight on her right leg. While walking one day, I asked if they knew Mr. and Mrs. Minato were Burakumin.

They both knew because of the area we were in. "I don't understand why people still look down on the Burakumin." I was irritated. "Who segregated them to begin with?"

"It was the shogun's order," said Ko. "Stupid!"

Hideyo said, "We cannot change our past or the fact that people will act in a certain way. However, the Kawashima children *can* become a few drops of water in the ocean and make ripples that will spread humanity."

PART THREE

TWENTY MONTHS AND ONE AUTUMN DAY

Once Sumiko had spread the word that I lived with the Burakumin, the students stayed away from me completely. I promised myself, The day will come when I will prove how wrong they were, and they will be very sorry. I was glad to be with Mr. and Mrs. Minato.

With bright persimmon trees heavily laden and pampas grasses reaching to the clear autumn sky, the Minatos taught Ko and me how to make straw slippers. They said we must make many pairs for Father and Hideyo. "There is plenty of straw in our neighbor's fields."

When I was in my junior year, in December 1948, I received a full scholarship from Sagano to go to Kyoto University to study in an experimental course called the English Village Program. There were thirty-five students gathered from the government-run schools in Kyoto.

A slender, medium-tall, blond-haired, piercingly blue-eyed, white-skinned, elegant professor, Francis P. White, conducted the class, but none of us understood him. He did not speak Japanese and we did not know how to converse in

English. What English I'd learned at Sagano came from reading sentences in the English reader books, "Rip Van Winkle" or *Oliver Twist*, and translating with the help of the dictionary. The professor pressured us into conversational English. We studied in the evenings and on Saturday afternoons. Because we were not allowed to speak Japanese once we entered the village, the village students did not speak to one another. Many dropped out.

"How is your English class coming along?" asked Ko. "Have you made friends with anyone?"

"We cannot speak our national language, so none of us are talking," I said. "It is a mentally strenuous course. We have lots of homework."

"That's good."

"It's not good when I don't understand what the professor is saying. If only he was allowing us to speak Japanese." I sighed. "He is very severe that way. Every day we have fewer and fewer students."

"Don't you ever get the idea of dropping out. I can tell he is a kind professor."

"What?" I yelled. "Kind?"

"Don't be so dumb. Kindness comes from a severe life-style," said Ko. "You said he is severe. But you will appreciate his severeness in the future. Besides, you are doubly dumb if you drop out of the university program. It is fully paid for by the government. This is the people's tax money. You owe it to them to finish the course."

In February 1949 I graduated from Sagano. Both Hideyo and Ko attended my graduation. When my name was called for the top honor, my brother and my sister, who were seated at the rear of the auditorium, followed Japanese custom and stood with me. I received the diploma and an outstanding-student award from the city mayor, who was on the stage. Instead of going directly back to my seat, I went to Hideyo and Ko who were still standing. I bowed to them ever so deeply to show my gratitude. Both of them shed tears of gladness. Just as I turned to go to my seat, Hideyo quickly patted my back as if to say, Good job!

After the ceremony, we were to take a class photograph. Everyone headed to the classroom, but when I was about to enter the room, I was stopped by Sumiko.

"Do us a favor—stay out of the class photo," said Sumiko. "We do not want a four-legged animal in our picture." I almost shoved her head through the windowpane. But *no* quickly came into my thoughts. I do not want to be in this mean, snobbish group any longer. I am not one of them.

I hastened back to Hideyo and Ko and I took them to the furnace room. For the first time Mr. Naido and my family met. Both Hideyo and Ko bowed to Mr. Naido for the many kindnesses he had bestowed on their Little One over the past four years.

Ko presented him with a summer kimono that she had sewn, and I gave him a cushion I'd made so that he could relax when he took his break on the furnace-room tatami mat.

"I am going to miss your sister," said Mr. Naido slowly, without a stutter. "This is the congratulations." He handed me an envelope. It contained ten yen! When I accepted it, sensing this would be the last time I'd see him, my chest tightened and I could not speak. I bit my lips and swallowed some lumps in my throat. To show him my deepest appreciation, I enveloped my hands over his for a long time. His tears ran down his face and dropped onto mine.

Though I had graduated from Sagano, I still had to study at the university's English Village for another year. I was hired as a professor's helper in the research department. On many Sundays I helped Mr. Maki with his fieldwork in exchange for rice or vegetables that he could not sell.

Hideyo kept two jobs and finally paid the hospital and the doctor's bill in full. From then on he handed his earnings to Ko to manage. He also faithfully kept on fixing Mr. and Mrs. Minato's house. "This is a never-ending job," Hideyo liked to say, smiling. "We may have to stay here for the rest of our lives."

Hideyo urged Ko to start taking classes at Seian University like she did before the fire, but

Ko said she wanted to save and buy some material to make kimonos for Father. "I can go back to school anytime," said Ko. Because she could not sit on the floor in Japanese fashion, Hideyo made her a table and a chair. She sewed steadily for her customers. She even made Father a futon from the ones that Mrs. Minato had given us when she left the hospital.

Whenever Ko was tired of sewing, she worked in the flower garden. She would sit on the ground, extending both legs, and scoot around to plant the seeds and weed. Mrs. Minato told Ko to use dried chicken manure for the garden. So it was my job to gather it from Mrs. Kinoshita's henhouse.

"We will have plenty of flowers for Mother's altar." Ko smiled. "I'd better teach you to make flower arrangements."

When Mrs. Kinoshita's hens stopped laying eggs, she asked if Hideyo, Ko, and I would help ready the chickens for market.

"I cannot twist hens' necks!" I protested, feeling afraid.

She said she'd felt the same way at first. She picked up a hen and twisted its neck and dipped it into hot water. She then showed me how to pluck the feathers. "Can you do this?"

So Mr. and Mrs. Kinoshita twisted the necks, Hideyo dipped the dead birds in the hot water, and Ko and I did the plucking. When the job was done, Mrs. Kinoshita gave us a naked hen to take home and said, "This is for you, and thanks."

That evening, Ko made sukiyaki for our supper. "I bet Father is hungry for sukiyaki," I said. "We must make it for Father when he comes home."

When I graduated from the English Village Program in the spring of 1950, there were only four students left, but we were able to do simultaneous translation from Japanese to English.

Though twenty full moons shone and faded, Father did not return. We wondered if the Russians had tricked us and killed Father soon after he'd written that letter. But we kept sending return postcards to Father's birthplace. By this time the construction company was working in a different area, but Hideyo made a weekly trip to Maizuru to post Father's name papers on the refugee-center wall.

Ko thought I now had enough to buy a secondhand pair of shoes. I went to a shoe shop and tried on the ones I had yearned for. But my feet had grown and the shoes were too small. Because I had been using Ko's shoes all this time, and Ko wore straw slippers when we took our evening walks, I decided to buy her a good pair of secondhand shoes. I showed a man what I had on and asked him if he had a slightly larger size. He did not. Then he brought out a dusty pair of men's brown leather shoes. They looked like new and the leather was soft.

I asked the man, "If they do not fit my sister, may I return them?"

"Of course," he said. "But it is best to bring your sister here so that I can find her a pair that fits."

"She cannot walk far. The shoes will be a surprise for her, so please polish them well for me."

When I gave Ko the present, she was taken by surprise and could not speak for a few moments. "Try them on," I said. "They will look good on you!"

"You do stupid things, sometimes. Take them back."

I told Ko the pair I wanted was too small and her old shoes fit me fine. "Please, at least you can try them on," I begged. I helped her stand and let her try on the pair. They were slightly big. "Wear double socks!" I said.

Ko had closed her eyes and was admiring the new shoes by putting them against her cheek to feel the softness of the leather. "Thank you, Little One! I treasure these," said my sister, smiling.

One bright autumn day when the huge red-tailed dragonflies dropped their shadows on the ground, we received the postcard we'd been longing for. It came from Father's birthplace. Father's letter soon followed. He said he would be arriving in Kyoto on Sunday, on the express train, at four-thirty in the afternoon.

We were all excited! But how were we going to break the news of Mother's death? Who would tell him?

"Not I," said Ko.

"Me either!" I shook my head. We both looked at Hideyo.

"I cannot do the job," said Hideyo. "I know he will be heartbroken."

Right up until that Sunday morning, we were discussing how to tell him the sad, sad news.

Finally, Hideyo suggested that as soon as Father got off the train, I should go to greet him. He would notice right away that Mother was missing. Ko, holding Mother's urn to her chest, would welcome Father. Then Hideyo would not give Father a chance to become sad. He would greet him cheerfully, "Well! Father! You made it! Welcome home!"

Ko and I cheered this splendid idea. To welcome Father, Ko decorated our eight-tatami-mat room with an elegant flower arrangement. I picked almost all the rest of the flowers from the garden for Mother's altar, where the precious family sword was always kept. Hideyo repaired the Minatos' wooden hot tub so that Father could bathe and relax. Mr. and Mrs. Minato trimmed their bamboo bushes, and I swept the narrow walkway. I even polished my shoes, smearing black crayon on the tips where they were worn.

The special Sunday arrived. Hideyo, Ko, and I stood on the train platform. I had never carried good feelings about the train station, but the extreme happiness of Father's return wiped away my bad thoughts. Ko had wrapped Mother's urn in a thin bath towel. She held it to her chest with both hands. Passersby, following Japanese tradition, bowed slightly to express their sympathy.

At 4:30 exactly, the train pulled into the station. My heart was beating loudly with joy. "I am excited!" I said. Both Hideyo and Ko nodded as if they understood my feelings, but they looked nervous. This was the last stop for the train. All the passengers were getting off. I searched for Father. I did not see him. Many travelers went by. Still no Father.

"Father did not come," I said in disappointment, looking at Hideyo. His eyes were searching for Father.

"There he is!" Hideyo pointed.

I looked in that direction. There were a few male passengers coming toward us, but they did not look like Father.

"I still don't see Father!"

"He is coming. Go greet him, Little One!"

"Where?"

"Over there! He is walking slowly, with crutches! Hurry! Go! Go greet him!"

I saw a feeble old man. His shoulders were slumped, his hair thin and white. He carried a shabby burlap bag, and his head was bent to see where he was walking.

"You mean that tired, feeble old man?"

"Shut up! Go, Little One, go!" Hideyo urged. I went a few steps forward, but I could not recognize him. I turned to Hideyo.

"He is not Father!"

"He is! Do what I tell you!"

I went very close to look at the old man.

The old man lifted his head. He studied me for a couple of seconds. I stared at him, wondering, Is this Father?

"Ah! Little One! My! You have grown so much!"

Only my family called me Little One. Still, I could not believe that this sick, old, weary, feeble man was my father. He gave me a huge smile. Hideyo poked my side, urging me to greet him.

"Welcome home, Honorable Father!" I said, bowing.

He nodded and smiled. He then leaned on his crutches, opened his shirt pocket and pulled out a brown comb. It had been given to him by Mother as a New Year's present many years ago. As he combed my hair, he kept on saying how much I had grown.

I moved beside Father so that Ko could welcome him. She bowed deeply to him without words. Father saw what Ko was holding on her chest.

"Is this Saki?" he asked. Saki was Mother's name.

Ko began sniffling and barely whispered, "I am sorry, Father."

Hideyo stepped forward quickly to aid Ko. "Welcome home, Father!" he said, bowing respectfully.

Father leaned on a crutch and extended his right hand to touch Mother's urn. He bit his lips. He tried hard not to cry and swallowed the lumps in his throat many times. Soon his eyes filled with tears. They streamed down his pale, wrinkled, tired face. "When did she go?" His voice was weak and trembling.

"Six years ago," answered Ko softly. "Shortly after she brought Little One and me safely to Kyoto. Mother died on November the nineteenth, nineteen forty-five."

"We are terribly sorry, Father," said Hideyo. "Please accept our deepest sympathy." We all bowed to Father.

Father kept on biting his lips, and his right hand, which was still touching Mother's urn, was trembling. He took out a handkerchief and wiped away his tears. Then he gently patted the urn. A memory came to me—Father patting my back when I pleased him. "You have done well!"

Father was still in tears, but he controlled his breathing. He then gave each one of us a gentle stare, and smiled. My brother, my sister, and I were warmed by his gesture. His voice trembled, but he spoke slowly and clearly. "I must not cry over what I have lost. I must give thanks for what Mother has left for me." He reached for my hand. "Now, Little One, show me the way to our home."

I put my hand in that familiar palm. I clasped his hand and looked into his eyes. Then magic happened. The tired, worn old man faded. I saw Father—my strong, wise, kind father. Almost as quickly, six years of hardship and heartbreak disappeared in the air. At long, long last, Father was home.

AFTERWORD

I still remember vividly, although it was a long while ago, that Father, Hideyo, Ko and I sat around the square table of the eight-tatami-mat room at the Minatos'. Mr. and Mrs. Minato also joined us. That evening Ko made sukiyaki to welcome Father. As we ate feathery grasses were gently blowing in the early autumn wind. A half-moon and sparkling stars sent us a bright light for the celebration. We were ecstatic.

Upon returning to Japan, Father retired from the government. He received a monthly pension that included payments for his six years of imprisonment in Siberia. Gradually our financial position improved but, in spite of our care, Father's health did not. There were deep scars on his neck and broad scars on his back. When I asked him, three different times, when and how was he beaten, he shook his head weakly and said, "It is not time to tell." But he assured me that the Communist system would never work. He gave it fifty years to fall. He longed to go to his birthplace, near where Mother was buried and where there was a hot spring.

When I graduated from the English Village Program at Kyoto University, I moved north with Father. Father had insisted that Ko resume her delayed education. As soon as Ko earned her master's degree from Otsuma University in Tokyo, she joined Father and me.

Until Father's death in 1966, Ko taught home economics at a high school and cared for Father. His last words to his children were, "Be kind to everyone. Spread your goodness wherever you go."

During the precious years with Father in 1952 through 1954, I worked at Misawa Air Force Base in northern Japan to help the household. Father's income could not keep up with Ko's and Hideyo's schooling expenses. Then I was hospitalized for acute appendicitis and underwent surgery. While in the hospital, I thought seriously about the most meaningful way to spend the rest of my life. Because a Buddhist monk had sharply refused to say prayers for the dead when Mother died, my young, fierce heart had refused to go to the temple for worship. I'd become a Catholic. I decided to enter a convent and help others as others had helped me. However, I planned to stay on the job until Father finished paying for my medical care and the school expenses.

One morning a base commander sent me to the coffee shack on the flight line to get a cup of coffee and cupcakes. Many soldiers were already there, waiting for food. As I walked to the end of the line, a young man in a flight jacket with a pistol hanging around his shoulder motioned for me to move in front of him. I shook my head. The pistol scared me to death. By the time my turn came, all the cupcakes were gone. I headed back to headquarters with only a cup of coffee. Then I was stopped by the young man in the flight jacket. Smiling, he handed me a sandwich and said, "I bought this for you. I was afraid everything would be sold out." I accepted the sandwich for the commander and thanked him. "What is your name?" he asked. I smiled at him but did not answer.

The next morning I had the same task. Again there was a long line of soldiers. That morning I was due at the courthouse by 10 A.M. for translating work; I was afraid I could not make it if I stood last in line. So when yesterday's young man motioned for me to stand in front of him, I accepted with a bow.

During the lunch hour, a telephone rang. A voice said, "Miss Kawashima! I want to get to know you! This is Donald Watkins." I answered politely, "I do not know you." "Yes you do! I bought you a sandwich yesterday, and today you were in front of me." I hung up the receiver quickly. A moment later he telephoned again. I was curious to know how he found out my name and where I worked. In a victorious tone he said, "It was easy! Japan is under occupation. I telephoned the labor office and got all the information!" I thought, what nerve!, and hung up the telephone.

At 4:30 P.M. Japanese personnel stopped working at the base. As I left the headquarters building to go home, I saw the persistent young soldier leaning against a telephone pole with a pipe in his mouth, waiting for me. He said, "Why are you so snobbish? I only want to be your friend. Don't you like me?"

I said, "I am not snobbish, but I do not wish to be friends with you." He wanted to know why. I told him it was because his country and mine had fought. "It's all right for your country to win, but not with atom bombs. I have seen many suffering victims. We became refugees and lost Mother." I almost cried, but I bit my lips.

"You are not friendly! Why are you working on an American base, then?"

"Simply money!" I said, coolly but politely. "Now please leave me alone."

The young man was quick to answer. "I want you to know, I did not start the war. Nor did you. We were unfortunately involved! Think about it." He turned around sharply and took off. All the way home, I thought of his words.

At suppertime Father listened carefully to what I had to say. I told him my feelings about the arrogant young American soldier. "Yoko!" Father said in a troublesome tone. Whenever my family called me Yoko instead of Little One, it was a sign of displeasure. Father's voice was soft but serious as he continued. "The young man was right. Yesterday's enemy must be today's friend. How can we keep peace otherwise? You must make a sincere apology when you see him again." One year later, with Father's permission and the blessings of Brother and Sister, we got married. Later we moved to the United States, where we still live. Our five children were born in America.

Hideyo remained at the Minatos' house and continued his work at the University Hospital. After he graduated from Kyoto Foreign Language University, he worked at Viatorian High School in Kyoto, becoming the head librarian. After marrying, he established his own home. When the United States was celebrating the Bicentennial, Hideyo brought his wife and their two sons, then 14 and 5, to see my family and Ko on Cape Cod. Though there had been telephone calls, correspondence, and packages between us, it was my first time seeing him personally in twenty-one years. He marveled at the size of North America, and we talked endlessly.

One week before he was due back in Japan, because I had been afraid to ask before and because I regretted my failure to learn about Father's prison treatment by the Communists, I came out with my question: "How did you escape from Nanam?" The sinking sun tinted the bay in crimson when he finished his story, and I heard the poignant cry of a whippoorwill in our woods. Just five months later, he joined Father and Mother in paradise.

Ko had come to join me in the United States in 1968. She lived with us for the next five years. Then she met and married George Patten and had 14 years of splendid marriage. During that time she established a dressmaking shop in Cambridge, Massachusetts. However, George developed Alzheimer's disease and is now in a nursing home. Ko volunteers at the facility, not only caring for her husband, but looking after other patients' needs as well. "Until George dies, I am his and he is mine," Ko has said.

When my first book, *So Far from the Bamboo Grove*, was published in the spring of 1986, I took two copies with me to Japan. One was for Mr. Naido and the other for Corporal Matsumura. It was my first visit to Japan since 1955. However, I learned that Mr. Naido passed away on the day my plane touched down on Japanese soil. I went to his small house in the forest not too far from Sagano. There I saw the wooden cart that he used to haul trash at the school. I gathered wildflowers and tied them with a long weed, then offered him the humble bouquet along with a copy of my book.

My friendship with Corporal Matsumura is still continuing. He and Mrs. Matsumura have a daughter named after me. Approaching ninety years of age, they live in Morioka with their son, Hajime, and his wife. I presented the corporal my book with a deep bow and said, "Anyone who reads this cannot help but love you." His son read the book to him with the help of a dictionary.

Later the corporal wrote, "Congratulations! But you are boasting about me. I am embarrassed. It was your attitude that made you a success as a human being. Keep it up!"

Mr. Minato died in 1975. Mrs. Minato, eighty-seven years old this year, still lives in the same house by the foot of Hiei Mountain. Two years ago, when she was helping her neighbor make rope, her right arm was caught in the machine and crushed. She had to learn to use her left hand to do everything. She wrote awkwardly, "I now understand what Miss Ko went through!" She continued, "I miss both of you. Come back again soon. The eight-tatami-mat room has been yawning for my friends." Hideyo visited and worked on her house often until his death.

My brother, my sister, and I emerged from the depth because we simply cooperated, accepted our responsibilities, and kept our dreams and hopes alive. I often shudder when I look back at my sad, painful past, but Hideyo and Ko gave me love and kindness in words and actions, as they had been shown by our parents.

I used to bring Father doughnuts from the market. Even now his voice echoes in my almost-deaf ears. "Your heart must never be like a doughnut, with a hole in the center. Fill it, and extend your kindness to all."

Yoko Kawashima Watkins
Massachusetts, 1994